Pam Hardy has w...... a. ........ .... ....ghtfully reflects on the balancing acts that all of us perform every day. I know that reading this will improve my sense of balance and I trust yours as well. In addition to being full of biblical wisdom, this book is a pleasure to read. Everything from writing style, to illustrative material, to opening and closing illustrations make this a satisfying read.

— *Tedd Tripp, Pastor, Author*
  *Shepherding a Child's Heart Seminar Presenter*


Pam Hardy's book, *Keeping Your Balance,* is excellent. It is full of God-honoring truths and practical application for our lives to *stay* balanced. I really enjoyed this book and highly recommend it either as an individual or group study.

— *Martha Peace*
  *Certified Biblical Counselor, Association of Certified Biblical Counselors*
  *Author of The Excellent Wife*


Maintaining balance in the Christian life is never easy but is absolutely necessary to advance in godliness. Pam Hardy does a remarkable job of helping women keep both feet on the ground in her book, *Keeping Your Balance.* This author is well-grounded herself, having had the blessing of sitting under sound preaching for decades. Pam draws upon this well of biblical knowledge and brings truth to bear on the various challenges facing Christian women. As ladies find themselves caught up in the many demands of busy lives and numerous responsibilities, Pam offers clear and competent counsel in her book that you will want to carefully study and practically apply.

— *Steven J. Lawson*
  *President, OnePassion Ministries*
  *Professor, The Master's Seminary*
  *Teaching Fellow, Ligonier Ministries*

I heartily recommend *Keeping Your Balance: Navigating Wisely through the Challenges of Life*. Pam Hardy has written an immensely practical book, full of wisdom and Scripture. She achieves her purpose of helping the reader balance seemingly opposite realities in seven key areas. Each chapter ends with a helpful summary of the negative effects of falling into either extreme. The study questions at the close of each chapter offer helpful suggestions, which help the reader dig deeper into the Bible to find the truth. I recommend Pam Hardy's book for personal study or group Bible studies.

— *Caroline Newheiser, Pastor's wife*
   *Certified Biblical Counselor, Association of Certified Biblical Counselors*
   *Assistant Coordinator of Women's Counseling,*
      *Reformed Theological Seminary, Charlotte, North Carolina*

Pam Hardy's writing showcases an example of the very balance she counsels. The wisdom that comes from knowing Christ and His Word, coupled with the experience of a long walk with the Savior, who was always the epitome of balance, brings color and depth to her sage advice, gentle cautions, and practical suggestions. Pam's charming personality is apparent in her sparkling writing style. I found the book personally challenging and will use it as a resource in my own counseling.

— *Dr. Clint Archer, Author, Senior Pastor*
   *Christ Fellowship Baptist Church, Mobile, Alabama*

Pam Hardy certainly accomplished her desire to show how to have balance in your Christian life. Don't be frustrated or discouraged if you feel like a failure in one or two areas of your life. Pick up this book, get a cup of coffee, find a quiet place, and learn how to be a gloriously balanced person!

— *Joyce Carpenter, Bible teacher, missionary, conference speaker*
   *First Baptist Church, Jacksonville, Florida*

Today we rarely hear the once-common expression "the balanced Christian life." Perhaps we are more interested in truth than in love, or in purity than in peace, or in zeal than in patience, or simply in what we accomplish rather than in who we have become. But eventually the importance of balance needs to dawn on us. In general in life, a lack of balance is usually a sign of immaturity (infants find it difficult), or of illness (mild or perhaps serious), or of the influence of an intoxicating substance. The same is true in following Christ. Balance is therefore not a deficiency but an indication that we are growing into maturity, being made well spiritually, and living under the control of the Spirit. So, three cheers for *Keeping Your Balance,* and hearty thanks to Pam Hardy for reminding us how essential it is, and for sharing her hard-won wisdom born out of her long and varied experience as a Christian, a mother, and the wife of a pastor. Full of shrewd observations and wise counsel rooted in Scripture, these pages are a safe guide to wholesome Christian living and a wonderful encouragement to grow in Christ-filled stability.

— *Sinclair B. Ferguson, Pastor, Author*
   *Teaching Fellow, Ligonier Ministries*
   *Chancellor's Professor of Systematic Theology, Reformed Theological*
      *Seminary*

This or that, now or later, good or best, yes or no? Such decisions are the connective tissue of our lives. Countless of these decisions are made daily, uniquely so in the lives of women desiring to please Christ. How a woman navigates these decisions generates spiritual equilibrium or throws her out of balance. Pam Hardy has crafted a resource here that is sure to ease unnecessary burdens, comfort conflicted consciences, and comfort troubled souls who long for stability. This book is wise, insightful, helpful, and *balanced.* It will be a well-worn volume by the women in our church.

— *Rick Holland, Pastor*
   *Mission Road Bible Church, Kansas City, Kansas*

Pam and her husband Carey are one of the godliest, most gifted, gracious, and gregarious couples I've ever had the privilege of knowing and serving alongside. Over the course of some thirty years, my wife and I have learned much from watching them *keep their balance* through the many challenges they have experienced in their life, family, and ministry. Pam lives what she writes, and in her book, she skillfully and winsomely blends biblical truth and practical advice that every woman, both young and old, needs to understand and apply in her life. I cannot recommend it highly enough!

— *Ken Ramey, Pastor-Teacher*
   *Lakeside Bible Church, Montgomery, Texas*

*Keeping Your Balance* is timely for the out-of-balance society we live in today. So much focus is on self that we forget God, which throws us off balance spiritually. Pam does a fantastic job of reminding us of our responsibility to read God's Word daily as our greatest resource for keeping our balance in this earthly life as a follower of Jesus. Having had the privilege of hearing her teach on the subject of trusting God, it is encouraging to know that some of that practical material is now in print within these pages. Scripture is found throughout each chapter, and Pam is clear and humble in her approach as she writes about the delicate balancing act of the Christian life. This book will definitely challenge its readers to keep your eyes fixed on the focal point, who is Jesus Christ our Lord, in order to keep your balance. He is the greatest example of all of a balanced Life!

— *Kelli Ramey, Pastor's wife, mother, teacher, singer*
   *Lakeside Bible Church, Montgomery, Texas*

I have long admired Pam as a wife, mother, and church-member, and have always treasured any opportunity to learn from her on any topic. This book is all the more valuable, given the relevance of the topic for anyone seeking to honor the Lord with their lives. Pam was such a blessing to myself and the women at Grace during her years here—I am grateful that a wider audience will now be able to benefit from her.

— *Patricia MacArthur*
  *Grace Community Church, Sun Valley, California*

You've undoubtedly heard the phrase, "It's just like riding a bike." Its meaning is usually connected to the idea that once you've learned how to do something—even if you haven't practiced for a very long time—it's easy to just hop back on and you'll generally navigate things again very successfully. Well, this isn't always true of course, and sometimes, just when you think to yourself, "No problem. I've got this," you may even end up "crashing and burning"! And this is most certainly the danger of navigating through the Christian life without proper practice in the matter of biblical balance. This is where Pam Hardy's book, *Keeping Your Balance,* comes in to help. What you now hold in your hands is a sure-footed guide on how to especially help Christian women navigate wisely through the dangerous challenges of life. With acute wisdom from God's Word, vivid illustrations from life's ups and downs, and a keen awareness of several crucial areas under examination, Pam strikes the right balance in each and every chapter. So, in a world fraught with massive imbalance, read on, my friend, so that you can truthfully and wisely say to yourself and others: "It's all a matter of balance, you know—just like riding a bike!"

— *Dr. Lance Quinn, Senior Pastor*
  *Bethany Bible Church, Thousand Oaks, California*
  *Fellow and Board Member, Assoc. of Certified Biblical Counselors*

No one likes to consider himself an extremist. But if the truth be told, many believers struggle with maintaining balance in the Christian life. With great clarity and sound biblical wisdom, Pam Hardy helps her readers identify the temptation toward extremism in several key areas of life and offers thoughtful corrections for returning to balance. This book is not a self-help pop-psychology book. The author provides rock-solid exegesis of biblical texts and displays a robust God-centered theology, which makes this book stand out from so much that dominates the current Christian book landscape in the category of sanctification. Whether for an individual study or a small group setting, I highly recommend this book.

— *Anthony Kidd, Pastor of Preaching*
  *Community of Faith Bible Church, South Gate, California*

Books on balance in the Christian life come and go, offering a few practical take-aways but little of the biblical depth and clarity we desperately need. In *Keeping Your Balance,* Pam Hardy has masterfully brought these elements together in a stimulating and scripturally rich volume. The practical helps are all here, born from decades of facing life in the trenches. Yet, the author's unmistakable wisdom and theological depth set this book apart. Each practical life challenge is keenly diagnosed at the heart level and skillfully treated with God's Word. Rather than mere lists of Bible verses to apply, Pam walks us through key passages, drawing out implications and helping us see the way to greater Christlikeness. You will find her transparency inviting, her counsel precise and insightful, and her discipler's heart compelling. This volume would be a powerful tool for strengthening body life in every church.

— *Jerry Wragg, Pastor*
  *Grace Immanuel Bible Church, Jupiter, Florida*

Although we live half a planet away, Pam Hardy has always been the favorite ladies' conference speaker of the women in our church. When you read *Keeping Your Balance,* you'll see why. Her seminars are a rare combination of biblical insight and practical sense. And now, with masterful skill, Pam has transferred those strengths to the written page. Rather than provide a "recipe" approach based on her own experience, Pam lays out with clarity and simplicity the biblical instruction on selected "balance" topics. She provides helpful warnings about steering too far to the left or to the right, and then allows you to apply the wisdom of Scripture in order to navigate your own specific situation. On behalf of the ladies in my church, thank you, Pam, for such an excellent book!

— *Dr. Joel James, Pastor-Teacher*
 *Grace Fellowship, Pretoria, South Africa*

Pam Hardy has a gift of weaving together thought-provoking principles, biblical theology, compelling stories, and excellent quotations in a practical and easy-to-digest format. Her choice of topics goes deeper than most family-church-work balance resources I've reviewed. I was also challenged and intrigued by the different ways this resource can be used in a variety of contexts.

— *Elaine Atchison, Director of Congregational Care*
 *Grace Community Church of Nashville, Tennessee*

There are some issues where we must choose 'either/or,' such as either sin or righteousness, either Satan's lies or God's truth. However, there are other matters that must be received as "both/ and," such as both church and family, both realism and optimism. Pam Hardy dishes up a plate full of practical wisdom on how to avoid turning "both/and" issues into "either/or" issues, and thus becoming imbalanced in the Christian life.

— *Dr. Joel R. Beeke, President*
 *Puritan Reformed Theological Seminary, Grand Rapids, Michigan*

To some extent, all of our lives lack balance. Well-researched, well thought out, and well written, Pam Hardy's book, *Keeping Your Balance,* is a Scripture-packed call to live a life of balance in a world of extremes. She helps us carefully examine our lives against Scripture in several key areas and provides real help. It's also a treasury of carefully-selected wisdom from many writers throughout the ages who lend their voices to the biblical call for balance. As I read this book, I recognized some areas in my own life where I need to improve. *Keeping Your Balance* will provide welcome help to believers who want to glorify God in this area.

— *Sheila Pennington, Women's Ministry Leader, teacher, and pastor's wife*
    *Countryside Bible Church, Southlake, Texas*


It is a pleasure for me to commend warmly and enthusiastically Pam Hardy's book, *Keeping Your Balance: Navigating Wisely through the Challenges of Life.* Writing out of a lifetime of experience as a pastor's wife and mother, Pam brings godly wisdom, a thoughtful, practical grasp of God's Word, and a deep appreciation of the insights of believers, ancient and modern, to her study. In an age of increasing imbalance, where evil is called good and good is called evil, Christians need to have their lives firmly imbedded in the balanced wisdom of God's Word. In eight brief chapters, each with a series of concluding questions for reflection and application, the author has provided believers with a sure guide to living the kind of life that will give godly poise to their lives and a godly luster to their gospel witness.

— *Dr. Ian Hamilton, Pastor, Author*
    *Professor of Church History at Westminster Presbyterian Theological Seminary in Newcastle, England*
    *Professor of Pastoral Theology at Greenville Presbyterian Theological Seminary in South Carolina*
    *Trustee on the Boards of the Banner of Truth Trust and G.P.T.S.*

# KEEPING

*your*
Balance

## Navigating Wisely through the Challenges of Life

PAM HARDY

Carpenter's Son Publishing

Keeping Your Balance
www.keepingyourbalancebook.com

Published by Carpenter's Son Publishing, Franklin, Tennessee

Published in association with Larry Carpenter of Christian Book Services, LLC
www.christianbookservices.com

Published in association with Patti McCoy Hummel, Literary Agent/Author benchmarkgroup1@aol.com.

Cover Image by Carey Drake, Illustrator

Edited by Adept Content Solutions

Cover Design and Interior Layout Design by Adept Content Solutions

Printed in the United States of America

978-1-952025-16-7

# CONTENTS

*To my husband Carey—*
*thank you for your constant love and support*
*and for making this journey with me.*


*To my children—*
*Christen, Nathan, Luke, and Catherine—*
*precious gifts to me from the Lord.*
*My simple prayer for you is that you will always*
*find your balance in Jesus.*

# ACKNOWLEDGMENTS

Writing a book is a significant undertaking and cannot be accomplished without the help and assistance of gifted people. I am extremely grateful to the following individuals for the valuable role they played in making this book a reality:

To Patti McCoy Hummel at Benchmark Group Literary Agency for believing in me and being a relentless encourager despite the many physical challenges she has dealt with during the writing of this book. You have become a cherished friend, and I am deeply appreciative of all you have done.

To Larry Carpenter and his team at Carpenter's Son Publishing for their skill and professional expertise in moving this book along one step at a time. Thank you for taking care of the countless details and enduring all my questions.

To Lori Martinsek and the wonderful people at Adept Content Solutions for their excellent work in the editing and design of the book.

To illustrator Carey Drake for his drawing of our "balancing woman" and especially for being so patient with all my minor adjustments. You did a great job of putting on paper what I had in my mind.

To Carolyn McGuire, who faithfully served in Women's Ministries at Grace Community Church, Sun Valley, California. While I have made many changes, the questions for reflection and application originally began with Carolyn in 2006. My thanks to you for your diligence and creativity.

To the godly men and women who have personally modeled for me a love for God and for Scripture over many years. I am still learning from your examples. I have also had the incredible privilege of sitting under a number of gifted Bible teachers during these years and I am indebted to each one of you for your impact on my life. Finally, there have been several dear friends at Twin City Bible Church who have prayed regularly for me during the writing of this book, especially during the final chapters. My heartfelt thanks for your faithful prayer support.

To my beloved parents, Ardis and Frances White, who are now safely with the Lord. It was an unspeakable blessing to grow up in a home with a father and mother who honored God and His Word and faithfully lived out what they believed. What they taught me is woven throughout this book.

To my grown children who have cheered me on throughout this entire process. Thank you for your love and continual encouragement.

To my husband Carey, who has wholeheartedly supported this book from the beginning. Your editing expertise and careful theological review of the various topics have truly been invaluable. You have brought clarity and precision to my thinking and have been a safeguard for me as I have sought to accurately convey doctrinal truth. On the practical side, thank you for sacrificially serving me in so many ways and especially for all the evenings you cooked dinner so I could write!

Above all, I am grateful to the Lord Jesus Christ, who showers me with His love and mercy each day. It has been such a joy to write about Him and, in the process, meditate on His perfections. If He chooses to graciously use this book to help someone, it will be because His Word is living and powerful and sharper than any two-edged sword (Hebrews 4:12). All praise and glory be to God who is more than sufficient for our every need (Romans 11:36; 2 Peter 1:3).

# FOREWORD

If prudence is the ability to apply biblical wisdom to life's challenges, then Pam Hardy shows herself to be a prudent counselor in *Keeping Your Balance*. She has an empathetic understanding of the way women are wired, and she artfully weaves together her Bible knowledge and winsome writing to create a powerful guide for every woman, young and old. This special book is a useful resource for women's ministries, one-on-one counseling, or for simply helping the reader sort through her home or work challenges. I give it a big thumbs-up!

—Joni Eareckson Tada
  *Joni and Friends International Disability Center*

# INTRODUCTION

This book was born many years ago when, as a young pastor's wife and mother of four children, I began to search for helpful material dealing with the issue of *balance* in life. In particular, I was looking for advice on how to juggle the myriad roles and responsibilities that periodically threatened to overwhelm me. I quickly discovered that there was very little written from a Christian perspective, which was a great surprise given that the need for balance pervades virtually every area of our lives. We inherently understand that balance is a good and necessary thing. Why else would we put so much effort into seeking to balance our time, our schedules, our careers, our bank statements? We know that a balance sheet is an essential tool used to evaluate financial health and that a balanced budget is a desirable goal. We also know that when balance is completely *lost* in some area of life, the result can be as bothersome as a broken dish, as painful as a broken bone, or as tragic as a broken relationship.

A dictionary defines *balance* as "a state of equilibrium."[1] Equilibrium is further explained as "a state of rest or balance between opposing powers and influences."[2] This brings to mind peaceful images of harmony, stability, and tranquility. Who doesn't desire a life characterized by these qualities? Yet because of our sinfulness and human frailties, what a frustrating and ultimately impossible task it is to achieve that desired balance. We strive mightily; we make the wisest choices we can. We inevitably find ourselves, however, erring on one side or the other. For example, confidence that lacks humility can become arrogance. A strong leader can deteriorate into a controlling dictator. Boldness can result in a dangerous slide toward foolishness. Honesty can be hurtful if not tempered by kindness.

As we deal with the consequences of our mistakes and miscalculations, we can begin to lose hope that we will ever achieve any semblance of the balance we yearn for. However, we must understand that in every area of life our hope is found in one place only, and that is in the person of the divine God-Man, the Lord Jesus Christ. He alone is our example of impeccable balance. As we study the Bible and what it reveals to us about the character of Jesus, we see in Him an excellence and a harmony of *Being* that is beyond our human comprehension. We observe His earthly ministry and are amazed at the perfect way in which He interacted with countless individuals throughout the Gospels. We are in awe of the exquisite tension He maintained between mercy and judgment, between grace and truth, between consolation and confrontation.

Kevin DeYoung makes these observations on the person of Christ in his book *Hole in Our Holiness:*

We see all the virtues of holiness perfectly aligned in Christ. He was always gentle, but never soft. He was bold, but never brash. He was pure, but never prudish. He was full of mercy but not at the expense of justice. He was full of truth but not at the expense of grace.[3]

In *The Incomparable Christ,* J. Oswald Sanders also paints a masterful picture of the perfectly balanced character of Jesus:

The character of our Lord was wonderfully balanced, with neither excess nor deficiency...It stands out faultlessly perfect, so symmetrical in all its proportions that its strength and greatness are not immediately obvious to the casual observer... Strong points necessarily presuppose weak ones, but no weaknesses can be alleged of Him. In the best of men there is obvious inconsistency and inequality, and...the greater the man, the more glaring his faults are likely to be. With Christ it was far otherwise. He was without flaw or contradiction.

Virtue readily degenerates into vice. Courage may degenerate into cowardice on the one hand or rashness on the other. Purity may slip into either prudery or impurity. The pathway to virtue is narrow and slippery, but in our Lord there was no deflection. Throughout His earthly life He maintained every virtue unsullied.

In speech as in silence, His perfect balance of character was displayed. He never spoke when it would have been wiser to remain silent, never kept silence when He should have spoken.

Mercy and judgment blended in all His actions and judgments, yet neither prevailed at the expense of the other. Exact truth and infinite love adorned each other in His winsome personality, for He always spoke the truth in love. His severe denunciations of apostate Jerusalem were tremulous with His sobs (Matthew 23:37). True to His own counsel, He manifested the prudence of the serpent and the simplicity of the dove. His tremendous inner strength never degenerated into mere obstinacy. He mastered the difficult art of displaying sympathy without surrendering principle...

...Most men are notable for one conspicuous virtue or grace—Moses for meekness, Job for patience, John for love. But in Jesus, you find everything. He is always consistent in Himself. No act or word contradicts anything that has gone before. The character of Christ is one and the same throughout...Its balance is never disturbed or readjusted.[4]

Here then is our divine example, found only in the person of our blessed Lord Jesus. In 1 John 2:6, believers are encouraged to "walk in the same way in which he walked" and yet we know that our sin keeps us from ever achieving perfection this side of heaven. But thankfully, the true child of God has a precious Helper. The indwelling Holy Spirit teaches us, leads us, convicts us, comforts us—in other words, He sanctifies us and helps us to mature in every area of life where we are willing to submit to Him. Because of Him, it is possible, thankfully, to attain *some* measure of that beautiful balance that we see in Jesus Christ.

It should be the goal of every Christian to grow in wisdom and discernment and in our ability to apply biblical truth practically in our lives. We need to make better choices in what we think, say, and do. We must learn to not waste time on worthless distractions but instead to invest in what is *worth* investing in. These are daily challenges in our lives, and we desperately need the assistance of the Spirit in our continual quest for balance. May we seek the Lord humbly, never forgetting that the ultimate goal of our lives is to simply bring glory to God in every way we can. We have been given one life to live on this earth. May we endeavor to live it as wisely as possible.

—*Pam Hardy*
 *July 19, 2020*

# ENDNOTES

1   Dictionary.com. (2019). "balance." *Dictionary.com*, based on the *Random House Unabridged Dictionary*. 2019. https://www.dictionary.com. Accessed September 12, 2019.
2   Ibid. "equilibrium."
3   DeYoung, K. (2012). *Hole in Our Holiness* (Wheaton, IL: Crossway), 47.
4   Sanders, J. O. (1971). *The Incomparable Christ* (Chicago, IL: Moody Press), 2–3.

*And everyone who competes [for the
prize] is temperate in all things.*
— 1 Corinthians 9:25 (NKJV)

*So, whether you eat or drink, or whatever
you do, do all to the glory of God.*
—1 Corinthians 10:31

Chapter 1
# BALANCE IS ESSENTIAL

The date was January 30, 1962. The place was the State Fair Coliseum in Detroit, Michigan, where the Ringling Bros. Circus was featuring the high-wire act of the legendary Wallenda family, or the "Flying Wallendas" as they had come to be known. Led by the patriarch of the family, a German man named Karl Wallenda, they were without question the greatest tightwire walkers in all of circus history. That night they were once again preparing to perform their most famous stunt, the amazing three-level pyramid. This trick consisted of four men standing in a line on the wire, yoked together by shoulder bars. On top of the shoulder bars stood two more performers, who in turn supported a woman who first sat in and then stood on top of a chair. The Wallendas never used a safety net, thinking it gave them a false sense of security and bred carelessness in the performers. They had done this dangerous stunt for fourteen years, successfully accomplishing it hundreds of times. But this night would be different.[1]

They carefully formed the pyramid and began to move out across the wire. Then the unthinkable happened. The first man on the wire, a young man named Dieter, lost his balance and fell to the floor, pulling down the two men immediately behind him, leaving one man standing alone on the wire. Karl and his brother fell to the wire from the second level of the pyramid, with Karl suffering a cracked pelvis in the fall. The girl who was at the top, Dieter's younger sister, fell on top of Karl. Although he was in great pain, Karl was able to hold her by the arm until a net could be brought beneath them. Of the three men who fell, Karl's son Mario was paralyzed from the waist down for the rest of his life. The other two men who plunged to the arena floor, Karl's young nephew Dieter and his son-in-law Richard, suffered fatal injuries and died soon thereafter. Seven thousand people watched in helplessness and horror as the tragedy unfolded before their eyes.[2]

*Balance* is a crucial skill! When we lose balance in some area of our lives, the results may not be quite as disastrous as they were for the Wallendas that night in Detroit, but they can still be damaging, not only to us personally but to all those around us. In this book, I want to discuss some of the most common areas of life where we are tempted to go to the extreme and therefore become unbalanced. Typically, when we realize that we've gotten off balance on some issue, our tendency is to make corrections and migrate back to a middle position. Too often, however, we overreact and swing past the middle and keep right on going. Then we find ourselves off balance and extreme on the *other* side.

I am constantly reevaluating my life to see whether I'm out of balance somewhere. Am I spending too much time here and not enough there? Am I pouring so much effort into something that I'm neglecting other things that are much more important?

In 1 Corinthians, we find an interesting verse related to this topic of balance. In this passage, the apostle Paul is using the analogy of a disciplined athlete to encourage excellence in life and ministry: "everyone who competes [for the prize] is temperate in all things" (9:24-25, NKJV). The word *temperate* conjures up ideas such as being moderate and exercising self-restraint in order to avoid excess or extreme. Common synonyms would include words like *self-controlled* and *balanced*. It is this self-control that Paul was encouraging when he urged believers "to live self-controlled...lives...in the present age" (Titus 2:12). The apostle certainly understood that temperance and self-control are essential to achieving our goals, and that principle is still as timely for us today as it was for the readers of Paul's day.

## THE ONE EXCEPTION

There is, however, one area of life where it is perfectly all right to be somewhat extreme, and that is in your love for the Lord Jesus Christ. In fact, your personal devotion to Christ should know no limits and no bounds.

In Deuteronomy 6:5, the children of Israel are given that great command to "love the Lord your God with all your heart and with all your soul and with all your might." Listen to King David in the Psalms as he exclaims, "I will give thanks to the Lord with my whole heart...I will be glad and exult in you; I will sing praise to your name, O Most High" (9:1-2). Hear Asaph as he cries out, "Whom have I in heaven but You? And there is nothing on earth that I desire besides You" (Psalm 73:25). There are countless verses in the Psalms that are focused exclusively on loving and praising Jehovah God (Psalm 27:1; 39:7; 42:1-2; 43:5; 54:4; 63:1-3; 111:1; 145:1-3; 146:2). Moving on to the book of Jeremiah, we take note of God's encouragement to the children of Israel: "You will seek Me and find Me, when you seek Me with all your heart" (29:13).

In the New Testament, what do we hear Paul say? "For to me to live is Christ" (Philippians 1:21). Later in the same book he states, "Indeed, I count everything as loss because of the surpassing worth of knowing Christ Jesus my Lord. For His sake I have suffered the loss of all things and count them as rubbish, in order that I may gain Christ" (3:7-8). Then in the book of Romans, the apostle writes his wonderful doxology: "For from Him and through Him and to Him are all things. To Him be the glory forever. Amen" (11:36).

Do these verses about our relationship with the Lord convey an attitude of indifference? Not at all. On the contrary, all through the Bible the scriptures confirm that we should be absolutely *passionate* about our relationship with God. Our problem is not that we love Him too much; our problem is that we love Him far too little. Do everything you can to stoke the fires of your love for Christ. Read His Word, study it, memorize it, listen to sound preaching and teaching, read good books, worship Him, praise Him, spend much time with Him in prayer, and continually set your mind on the character and the majesty of Almighty

God. In this one area, it is perfectly right to be consumed with wanting to know and love the Lord.

## THE CALL FOR BALANCE

In virtually every other category of life, however, the call is for self-control and balance. The purpose of this book, therefore, is to prompt us to look at some basic areas of life where we have a tendency to be extreme or excessive. Please note that as we consider these areas, I am not contrasting something good with something bad; instead, the areas being discussed are all *good* things in our lives. Yet even good things can become too important to us (1 Corinthians 6:12) and eventually develop into idols of the heart. Maintaining balance is therefore crucial.

While this book is not intended to provide the reader with an exhaustive list of categories, we will touch on many of the major issues that we deal with at one time or another. As we navigate through the various areas of life, it should become evident that some of the common counseling concerns that plague Christians are related to this problem of being out of balance. They have gone to the extreme in some area, and it's causing difficulties not only in their own lives but also in the lives of the people around them.

Each chapter will address a major category of life where all believers—and especially Christian women—can potentially be extreme on one side or the other. The first thing we will do is endeavor to determine the correct balance from God's Word. Then we'll discuss what it looks like when we find ourselves *out* of balance. I trust that the symptoms mentioned will help you identify problem areas in your own life and therefore ways in which you can grow.

*For Personal Reflection and Application*

## CHAPTER 1—BALANCE IS ESSENTIAL

1. Define the concept of balance in your own words and describe how you would desire this to look in your own life. Can you identify any areas that might possibly need your attention?

2. Read through 1 Corinthians 9:24-27 and note the race metaphor Paul uses to describe our earthly lives. What similarities and what differences do you see between this metaphor and your own life?

3. Look up the scripture references given that illustrate how the psalmists expressed their devotion to the Lord (Psalm 27:1; 39:7; 42:1-2; 43:5; 54:4; 63:1-3; 111:1; 145:1-3; 146:2). How do these scriptures challenge you in your own devotional time?

4. Summarize Philippians 1:21 and 3:7-8 in your own words. What are some of the practical steps you can take to increase your love for Christ?

# ENDNOTES

1    eLibrary. "Rulers of the Air.". http://ask.elibrary.com/printdoc. asp?querydocid=6525966@urn. Accessed March 1, 2003

2    The Flying Wallendas. "History." http://www.wallenda.com/ history.html. Accessed February 15, 2003.

*Honor your father and your mother...*
— Exodus 20:12

*...train the young women to love
their husbands and children...*
— Titus 2:4

*...do not provoke your children to anger,
but bring them up in the discipline
and instruction of the Lord.*
—Ephesians 6:4

*...to equip the saints for the work of ministry,
for building up the body of Christ...*
—Ephesians 4:12

*Having gifts that differ according to the grace
given to us, let us use them...do not be slothful
in zeal, be fervent in spirit, serve the Lord.*
—Romans 12:6, 11

*To each is given the manifestation of
the Spirit for the common good.*
— 1 Corinthians 12:7

## Chapter 2
# FAMILY AND MINISTRY

Being raised in a home with loving parents and close family relationships is a blessing from God for which I will always be profoundly grateful. The importance of family—my immediate family as well as my grandparents and other relatives—was instilled in me from my earliest days. My husband also experienced the security of growing up in a stable and close-knit family. In addition to this, we were both raised in the context of committed involvement in a local church, with my husband even growing up in a pastor's home. After we married, my husband eventually entered the ministry and so our four children grew up in a pastor's household as well. Both these entities, the family and the local church, have therefore been major influences throughout my entire life. And that is why we will begin our discussion with the balance between *family* and *ministry*. This is a necessary balance for all Christian women, especially if you are actively involved in serving others in your church. For me personally, since I have been a pastor's wife for a long time, this has always been one of my biggest struggles. Perhaps it is a struggle for you as well.

It goes without saying that both family and ministry are wonderful blessings from the Lord. And as believers, we have obligations in both these areas. If you are a wife or mother, the Bible has much to say about your responsibilities to your husband and children. The New Testament books of Titus and 1 Timothy tell us that Christian women are to "love their husbands and children...working at home" (Titus 2:4-5); they are to "marry, bear children, manage their households" (1 Timothy 5:14). In Proverbs 31, we meet the excellent wife who "looks well to the ways of her household" (31:27).

As members of the body of Christ, however, we also have a responsibility to minister to others within the body. In Romans 12:3-8 and 1 Corinthians 12:4-11, we are told that we have all been given spiritual giftedness that we are to use in serving our brothers and sisters in Christ. There are also many verses in the New Testament dealing with what are called the "one anothers" of Scripture. For example, we are told to love one another; to forgive one another; to exhort, to edify, to admonish, to restore one another; and to provoke one another to love and good works. Yet it's utterly impossible to do these things if we are not involved in the lives of the other believers around us.

It is therefore quite clear that the Bible validates the importance of both family and ministry. The problem is that each can require a considerable amount of time, and yet there are only twenty-four hours in a day. Since we have to make choices, finding the right balance between the two can be very difficult. We must go to the Word of God to find the right order of our priorities.

## THE PRIORITY OF THE FAMILY

*The Biblical Order*

Scripture clearly teaches that we must never put anything or anyone above our relationship with God and that includes our family. "I am the Lord your God...you shall have no other gods before me" (Exodus 20:2-3). An idol of the heart can be anything that we love or worship more than God, and we must guard against this (Colossians 3:5). In Colossians 1:18, the apostle Paul declares in no uncertain terms the place that Christ deserves: "that in everything he might be preeminent." Therefore, our relationship with God (i.e., the vertical realm of our lives) must be above all else. When we talk, though, about the horizontal realm, which consists of our human relationships, the Bible lays out a very definite order. After your relationship with the Lord, if you are married, the husband–wife relationship is *the* priority human relationship. As it says in Genesis 2:24, "A man shall leave his father and mother and hold fast to his wife, and they shall become one flesh." This verse in Genesis testifies to the singular nature of the marriage relationship. I am not *one flesh* with anyone else in the body of Christ. I am not one flesh with my parents or my children. I am only one flesh with my husband.

Another passage that testifies to the uniqueness of marriage is found in Ephesians 5:25-31. Here the relationship between a husband and wife is said to be a picture of Christ and His church. As with the one flesh imagery, this symbolic picture is not applied to any other human relationship.

### Don't Forget the Kids

So where do our children fit into this picture? In 1 Timothy 3:4-5, Paul tells us that an elder "must manage his own household well, with all dignity keeping his children submissive, for if someone does not know how to manage his own household, how will he care for God's church?" This passage outlines the requirements for an elder, and obviously, not every man will hold that office. Yet the elders are to be an example for the rest of the church. They are to set a standard that the other men are to respect and emulate. The implication is that all Christian parents are to take their roles in the family seriously.

We find another well-known verse in the letter to the Ephesians: "Fathers, do not provoke your children to anger, but bring them up in the discipline and instruction of the Lord" (6:4). We are not to frustrate or exasperate our children but instead are to put time and effort into raising them and teaching them to honor God. When you couple these passages with the instructions to mothers to "love their children" and "look well to the ways of their households," it becomes very clear that the family is a priority. We have a huge responsibility to our children simply because they are the children that the Lord has given to *us*. These scripture passages, along with many others, emphasize that our relationship with our children is very significant and thus it has a bearing on our testimony to those around us.

Since Scripture acknowledges the importance of the family, we must be careful to *never* elevate ministry to people outside the family above ministry to our own families. If we are neglecting our God-given responsibilities as a wife or as a parent, we will probably begin to see the effects in our family. When we are so busy that we can't seem to find the time to invest in our own children, it will inevitably impact the home.

This is particularly critical when parents are involved in full-time Christian ministry because of the increased ministry-related demands on their time. Pastors especially need to carefully guard time with the family and keep it a priority. Thankfully, there are many church activities where the whole family can participate together, and these are to be encouraged as much as possible. If a pastor's ministry obligations, however, are consistently allowed to interfere with or take precedence over his time and activities with his wife and children, this can become a serious problem. The danger is that, especially for the children, it can gradually lead to resentment and a diminished love for the local church and its people. We never want our children to feel like other people—especially those at the church—are more important to their mother and father than they are. We want our children to love the church and be committed to it. We do not want them to ever see the church as the reason that Mom and Dad were too distracted or too busy to be there for them in times of need.

Whether we are talking about a pastor's family or not, all of us will inevitably face situations in the local church that are out of our control, such as deaths, accidents, and family crises. In those times, the entire family may need to sacrifice in order to minister to others in need. But there should also be times when our children see us sacrificing for them. Sometimes it will be necessary to be with large groups of people; at other times, however, we need to make certain our children have us all to themselves without having to compete with other people for our attention. And the younger they are, the more essential that is. As children get older, they will mature in their understanding of life and ministry and their ability to share their parents with other people.

The overall guiding principle is, in the midst of all your many ministry activities and obligations, to make sure you carve out substantial time to be with your family and no one else. This applies once again to all families, whether the parents are involved in full-time ministry or simply active members of a local church. Do as many things together as you can: times of worship at church, mealtimes, family devotions, prayer times, game nights, movie nights, various church, school, and sports activities, holiday celebrations, and special trips and vacations. Just do life together! To the best of your ability, enthusiastically support your children in their endeavors and interests. If they are athletic, be at every game you can; if they are involved in the fine arts, go to every concert or performance possible. When you are not there to cheer them on, it should be the exception rather than the rule. You will never regret one moment you spend trying to strengthen your relationship with your children and encourage them. Pour as much time and effort as you can into building the type of family that they will enjoy and treasure.

*Keeping Our Priorities in Order*

The bottom line is this: if we have children, they must know beyond a shadow of a doubt that they hold a very special place in our hearts. Of course we need to love other people, especially the people in our church. We need to minister to others and be involved in their lives, but our children *must* have the assurance that they are a priority. They have been entrusted to us by the Lord. We have been given the responsibility to love them, teach them, and raise them in the knowledge of Him (Ephesians 6:4). Therefore, we must guard against being so involved with everyone else that we don't give our own children the time and attention they need. Sadly, we are sinners, and we fall short in many ways as parents; despite our best intentions, there are no perfect parents, and there will definitely be times when we fail. In light of this, one of the most meaningful things we can do is regularly let our families know how deeply we love them. It is vital that our children can look back on their growing-up years and remember our unfailing love and the fact that we wanted to spend time with them. Never sacrifice your long-term relationship with your children for relationships that often end up being short-term. For one reason or another, many of the people who are in our lives today will not even be there in ten years. But our children, those children that the Lord has given to us, will likely be there for a long time.

*What if I'm Single?*

If you are unmarried, this is a unique opportunity to serve Christ and other believers. You should therefore seek to maximize this opportunity. Yet even here there is still a balance since you may have parents, siblings, or extended family to consider. If your family members do not know the Lord, you may possibly find yourself feeling closer to many of the people in your church. If this is the case, remember to still value the family where God placed you and bear in mind that your testimony of love and concern for them is crucial. Do your utmost to stay actively involved in these relationships. Never allow your ministry to your church family to lessen your attempts to minister to your earthly family.

## THE RESPONSIBILITY OF MINISTRY TO OTHERS

*Don't Forget Other People*

As we have established, family is tremendously important. On the other hand, we still have to guard against being selfish and drifting into the "us four and no more" mindset. We must be careful not to become child-centered or make idols out of our children. This can happen when we fall into the trap of allowing everything to revolve around them in an unhealthy way, leading us to neglect our responsibilities in other key areas of life. We also need to be aware of the subtle temptation to be so absorbed with our own families that we simply don't have time to minister to anyone else.

Be intentional when it comes to the needs of the people around you, both believers and unbelievers. Reach out not only to the people in your church but also to your friends and neighbors who don't know Christ. Stay alert to the many ways you can use your abilities and gifts to serve others in your community. One of the surest paths to joy and contentment is to spend your life focusing on the needs of others rather than focusing on self.

### Are You Too Busy?

One thing to keep in mind related to this discussion is that we must never equate the well-being of our relationship with God with our busyness in ministry outside the home. They are not the same thing. There are times in life when we are completely committed to the Lord and our relationship with Him is strong and healthy; and yet for the people closest to us, the wisest thing we can do for a certain period of time is to take a step back in our ministry duties. What happens far too often, unfortunately, is that people get so busy in outside ministry that it begins to take a toll on their families.

### The Changing Seasons

As you juggle your many responsibilities, recognize that there are different seasons of life. At times, you will have much greater capacity for outside ministry than at other times. Especially if you are a mother with babies and small children, they *must* be your priority. The Lord has sovereignly given these children to *you*, and that is a massive responsibility. But do not think that you cannot be involved in ministry during those seasons. Praying for other people is ministry. A phone call, making a meal for someone—that's ministry. In this time of life with small children, your wisest approach is to focus on service that can be accomplished in your own home and does not require large amounts of your time. Also, when you do minister to someone, always try to involve your children if possible. We want to teach them very early that we care about other people so they will see serving others as a natural part of life. Ministry is both a privilege and a joy and it is our responsibility to model that to our family.

As your children grow up and eventually leave the home, you will gradually realize you have more freedom for outside ministry. During my years as a pastor's wife, I have been involved in a number of different church ministries. Unfortunately, there were times when the obligations piled up, and I allowed myself to become over-committed outside the home. I was out of balance. I recall specific moments in time when I had to drastically pull back and simplify my schedule for the good of my family.

*Your Primary Realm of Discipleship*
Though I have engaged in long-term discipleship rela-tionships with other women through the years, at times I have felt guilty that I've not done more in this regard. But do you know what the Lord finally helped me to understand? For many, many years, I was involved in four very long-term discipleship relationships: my *children* are my main disciples! They are the disciples that God has entrusted to me and to my husband. What a tragedy if I am so busy and so distracted with all the ladies at my church that I don't have enough time for my *most* import-ant disciples: my own children.

## DON'T FORGET YOUR HUSBAND

Finally, if you are a wife and a mother, I want to mention a "sub-balance" here that is related to the family, and that is the balance between our husband and our children. As a mother who has raised four children, I realize at times they can truly be all-consuming. The years when all the children are still living at home are arguably the busiest and most demanding years of our lives. At times, we can feel like we barely have time to breathe. And it's easy at those times to be so focused on the children that we have no time or energy left for our husbands. I can remember a few times when my husband came home from work and I was so exhausted that I wanted to just toss the kids to him at the door and go straight to bed! My encouragement to you is to simply do your best to reserve some energy for interaction with your husband. Even something like a quiet talk on the couch after the kids are in bed can go a long way. Never forget that the husband–wife relationship is still the foundational relationship in the family, and it must not be neglected, no matter what season of life we may be in.

## THE EXTREMES

So when we get out of balance in this area of family and ministry, what does it look like? What are the symptoms that can surface in our lives? If you are too extreme in your emphasis on the *family*, here are some common signs:

- A self-centered focus on the family
- A tendency to idolize your children (making your life revolve around them)
- Neglect of ministry to those outside the family
- Lack of commitment and reliability in your local church body

If you are out of balance on the side of *ministry*, you may see these issues:

- Neglect of your responsibilities to and within your family
- Challenges with children and family that result from a lack of proper attention to family matters
- A lack of love for the church among your children

This is without question a difficult balance to maintain. Be willing to take a step back and evaluate how you are doing in this category. If you are single, ask others in the church if they have any concerns about you, your family, and your ministry involvement. If you are married, ask your spouse for helpful insights. Be willing to humbly receive input about these critical aspects of life and always pray for God's wisdom and direction in the choices you make. The balance between family and ministry is of utmost importance and you will be glad you listened to the objective viewpoints of those around you.

## For Personal Reflection and Application

### CHAPTER 2—FAMILY AND MINISTRY

1. How do the principles in this chapter apply to those who are not married? What are the responsibilities of those who are single to their families?

2. What does God tell us in Genesis 2:24 and Ephesians 5:22-23 about how a Christian husband and wife are to relate to one another? What are a wife and mother's priorities according to Titus 2:4-5 and 1 Timothy 5:14?

3. Summarize the parental responsibilities described in Deuteronomy 6:5-7 and Ephesians 6:4. If you are a parent, in what way do these verses personally challenge you?

4. Study Romans 12:3-8 and 1 Corinthians 12:4-27. How are the members of the body of Christ similar to the members of a physical body? Taking into account these similarities, what should be our prevailing attitude as we minister to one other?

5. We find many of the "one anothers" of Scripture in the following passages: John 13:34; Romans 15:14; Galatians 5:13; 6:1-2; Ephesians 4:2,32; Colossians 3:16; 1 Thessalonians 5:11;

Hebrews 3:13; 10:24-25; 1 Peter 5:5; and 1 John 1:7. Ponder these responsibilities that we have to our brothers and sisters in Christ and identify where you need to grow.

6. Describe a time when you had to say no to maintain a proper balance between your ministry to your family and ministry to other believers.

*"…If anyone would come after me,*
*let him deny himself and*
*take up his cross daily and follow me."*
—Luke 9:23

*…training us to renounce ungodliness*
*and worldly passions, and to live*
*self-controlled, upright, and godly*
*lives in the present age…*
—Titus 2:12

*For freedom Christ has set us free…*
—Galatians 5:1

*For you were called to freedom, brothers.*
—Galatians 5:13

*…God, who richly provides us*
*with everything to enjoy.*
—1 Timothy 6:17

## Chapter 3
# SELF-DENIAL AND LIBERTY

Many well-known lines from the plays of William Shakespeare have endured for centuries. One of the most widely known quotes is found in Hamlet's soliloquy in Act 3, Scene 1 of *Hamlet*. As the tragic prince agonizes over the nature of life and whether living or dying is best, he begins his speech with these famous words: "To be, or not to be: that is the question."

While this pithy statement has been interpreted and applied many different ways, one reason for its fame is that it deals with such a profound philosophical concept—that of existence and the consummate choice "to be" or "not to be." And while some would consider this existential question to indeed be pivotal, there is another issue in life that is arguably as profound and far-reaching: the crucial choice "to do" or "not to do." Our lives confront us daily with decisions about what we do and don't do, and this ushers us into our next area of balance: the balance needed between *self-denial* and the exercise of allowed *liberty*. This topic is a weighty one since it involves the choices we make every single day. We must decide what we partake of and what we don't, what we watch and what we don't, what we invest time and effort in and what we don't.

Without question, the concept of self-denial is an essential aspect of our Christian life from the very first moment of salvation. In Luke 9:23, our Lord says, "If anyone would come after me, let him deny himself and take up his cross and follow me" (see also Matthew 16:24; Mark 8:34). Implicit in the concept of bowing our knee to the Lordship of Christ is the denial of self and surrender to God's will in and for our lives.

We understand that to live a holy, godly life, there are many things we need to say no to. We are instructed in Titus 2:12 to deny "ungodliness and worldly passions" and "live self-controlled, upright, and godly lives in the present age." The book of 1 Corinthians encourages us to discipline our bodies and keep them under control (9:27). Of course, it goes without saying that we want to avoid obvious sin. Elsewhere in 1 Corinthians, however, the apostle Paul tells us there are even good things we may need to deny ourselves because they are not helpful for us (6:12). So the Christian life is undoubtedly a life of self-denial.

We find a blessed balance, though, in the letter to the Galatians. In the fifth chapter, Paul tells us to stand fast in our liberty and not "submit...to a yoke of slavery" (5:1, NKJV). Then just a few verses later in the same chapter, he reminds the reader that "you have been called to liberty" (5:13, NKJV). The Greek word for *liberty* is translated "freedom" in the English Standard Version, which further helps convey the full meaning of the term.

From these verses it's quite clear that along with self-denial, we have also been granted freedom in Christ. Paul reinforces this thought when he reminds us that God "richly provides us with everything to enjoy" (1 Timothy 6:17) Other passages such as Romans 14 provide additional insight into how believers should handle their freedoms. This chapter also stresses the necessity of always operating in love toward our brothers and sisters in Christ (14:14-19). In Colossians 2:16-23, we again find Paul touching on this matter of self-denial and liberty. Here he cautions Christians against judging each other and being enslaved by legalistic rules and regulations that have no direct or overt basis in Scripture.

## THE GREAT DIVIDE

Sadly, the issue of Christian liberty is a controversial one that believers have been arguing about for a very long time. But the controversy simply points to the vital need for balance in this area. Here is what lies at the heart of the matter: we absolutely have liberty in Christ, but we cannot ever let that liberty lead us into sin. In Galatians 5:13, we are told that we are called to freedom, but it also plainly admonishes us not to use our freedom "as an opportunity for the flesh." In his first epistle, we also find the apostle Peter addressing the exact same issue with this helpful exhortation: "Live as people who are free, not using your freedom as a cover-up for evil, but living as servants of God" (1 Peter 2:16). So Scripture is clearly not the source of the controversy surrounding this subject. Instead, the source of contention is found primarily in the many different opinions among Christians as to whether a particular liberty is allowed and also in the unwillingness of some to exercise wise restraint in their freedoms.

*Perils on Either Side*

Self-denial and liberty are necessary complements to one another in the Christian life, yet you can so easily go to the extreme on either side. Believers who put excessive emphasis on their freedoms may think they are innocently enjoying their liberty in Christ. As time passes, however, they can unfortunately digress to the point of minimizing the importance of holy living and then even falling into blatant sin. We must always guard against being brought under the power of sin (1 Corinthians 6:12).

On the other hand, Christians who are focused on self-denial can quickly sink into the mire of self-righteousness and become proud of all those things they are denying themselves. They can potentially become enamored with their own self-control, and much like the Pharisees of Jesus' day, they actually look to these things for the righteousness needed to gain acceptance with God. The natural (and unfortunate) progression of this tendency is that these individuals often begin to judge their fellow believers by the standards they have put in place in their own lives. Sadly, all of this gives evidence not of genuine righteousness but of *self*-righteousness.

## THE SNARE OF LEGALISM

This fixation on self-denial that leads to self-righteousness is the essence of what many call *legalism*. In the Bible, the concept of legalism is generally related to the issue of salvation and the futility of thinking that we can somehow accumulate favor with God and earn our salvation through self-denial and good works. In contrast to this biblical usage, today when we characterize someone in common verbiage as being "legalistic," we are typically referring to the topic of *sanctification*. What is sanctification? The meaning of this word is derived from Hebrew and Greek terms that convey the idea of being "set apart" and "made holy." Progressive sanctification therefore has to do with growing spiritually to be more like Christ and thus more set apart for His purposes. In this chapter, we will be examining legalism as it relates to our sanctification.

Another common term for legalism is *works-righteousness*. Again, this is the mistaken belief that we can become *more* righteous in God's sight because of what we do and don't do. Yes, of course we need standards and we need to live holy lives. But remember, our good works do not in any way increase our acceptance with God. This is an incorrect understanding of the doctrine of justification, which deals with the subject of how we attain a right standing before God. A works-righteousness system is also a skewed approach to sanctification in which we seek to grow spiritually by focusing only on the externals and not on the heart. This is not a new problem. In Matthew 23, Jesus was once again confronting the self-righteous Pharisees and He addressed their hypocrisy with this scathing denunciation:

> Woe to you, scribes and Pharisees, hypocrites! For you are like whitewashed tombs, which outwardly appear beautiful, but within are full of dead people's bones and all uncleanness. So you also outwardly

appear righteous to others, but within you are full of hypocrisy and lawlessness. (23:27-28)

### His Righteousness, Not Ours

Our self-denial and our good works do not save us. And after salvation, they don't make us more acceptable to God. When we come to Christ in saving faith, He credits to us *His* righteousness. We have never possessed a righteousness of our own and never will. We will never be able to add anything at all to what Christ has already imputed to us. This is the essence of the gospel message—that we are saved, and kept saved, by God's amazing grace! John Piper echoes this:

> God accepts us on the basis of Christ's righteousness, not ours. To be sure, our progressive sanctification—our all-too-slow growth in Christlikeness—matters. It is the necessary evidence that our faith is real. But, oh, what a difference it makes to be assured, in the discouraging darkness of our own imperfection, that we have a perfect righteousness—namely Christ's.[1]

### Why the Gospel Matters

This is a reminder of the significance of the gospel and of what Christ accomplished for us by His perfect life and by His substitutionary sacrifice on the cross. We must never forget this. When we think on Him and ponder His atoning work on our behalf, we are motivated anew to obedience and good works. Yes, we embrace the obligation to obey the Lord's commands—an obligation that is inherent to being one of His followers and acknowledging His Lordship. But a robust appreciation for the gospel prompts a spirit of joy and thankfulness as we seek to obey. And this spirit of deep gratitude, along with the daily awareness of Christ's love for us and our love for Him, makes a world of difference not only in what we do but why and how we do it.

### The Older Brother Syndrome

Too often as Christians, we act like the older brother in the story of the prodigal son in Luke 15:11-32. He was not blatantly defiant like the rebellious younger brother. In fact, at least outwardly, he was compliant and cooperative—a model son! Yet all the while, as becomes evident later in the parable, he was harboring deep bitterness in his heart toward his father. He may have been obedient, but he did not love his father any more than his younger brother did. He certainly did not grasp the gracious love of the father for him. He was obeying for *himself*; he was obeying to gain acceptance with the father. In other words, he was obeying for all the wrong reasons.

The older brother in the story of the prodigal son in Luke 15 is a perfect picture of works-righteousness—doing things in order to gain favor with God and somehow accrue righteousness. The true gospel, however, tells us something completely different. When we throw ourselves upon God in humble repentance and faith, bringing nothing to Him but our utter helplessness, He graciously saves us. Then after salvation, as we live our lives, we must remember that there is still nothing we can do to become more righteous in our standing before Him. If we are truly regenerate, God has "made us accepted in the Beloved" (Ephesians 1:6, NKJV) and therefore our obedience proceeds not only out of a sense of duty but also out of profound love for our Savior. We don't obey in order to earn God's grace; we obey *because* of God's grace. The gospel operating daily in our lives is what rescues us from legalism.

### *Choices, Choices, Choices*

A companion thought in this discussion deals with what we actually choose to do and not do in our Christian lives. If we don't want to fall into legalism and the habit of judging other people, it is imperative that we learn to distinguish between *biblical* issues and what are commonly called *preference* issues. A biblical issue is one that is spelled out in Scripture as something clearly promoted or clearly forbidden, and there are plenty of these to be found. A preference issue, in contrast, is one that is not specifically encouraged or prohibited in Scripture. Sometimes we call these the "gray areas" of life, and there are plenty of these as well.

Many of our preferences, even our strong personal convictions, tend to be connected to externals (appearance, behavior, etc.) The list of these preference areas is a very long one. It can include outward appearance: Is it wrong to wear makeup? Can women wear pants? How long should a man's hair be? What about tattoos and piercings? It can involve entertainment: Should we watch television? Should we even *own* a television? Can we go to the movies? Which movies are allowed? Is a "G" rating permitted but nothing else? How about music? Christian or secular—can we listen to both or just one kind? And where do we draw the line within those music categories of what we can listen to and what we can't? What about types of schooling? Public, private, or homeschooling—which one is the *right* way? The world of politics is another volatile area where Christians can have diverse viewpoints. Who's right? Who's wrong? Who knows?

There are quite a few gray areas in which believers can hold to very different opinions. The danger here is that no matter what our beliefs might be, we have a natural tendency to judge those who disagree with us. It is essential, however, that we learn to respect the preferences and convictions of our brothers and sisters in Christ as we would want them to respect ours. Occasionally there may be times when we are compelled to humbly and lovingly speak the truth to another believer because we're genuinely concerned about an issue in their lives. Ultimately, however, we are not the judge (Romans 14:10). We must therefore learn to trust God to lead and guide in each believer's life and simply leave it with Him.

## Confusing the Issues

What leads us down the narrow path of legalism is when we take a preference issue and treat it (and fellow believers) as if it is a biblical issue. When a Christian begins to focus on externals and then also begins to judge others by those same criteria, this person is said to be "legalistic." So a danger of legalism as it relates to our sanctification is judging your own spirituality and that of other Christians by manmade rules that are not spelled out in scripture. And it is this legalistic judging that is then the perfect prescription for creating conflict between believers.

If we are honest, we must acknowledge that legalism is a constant temptation for each of us. Because we are flawed, sinful people, we all struggle at times with areas of legalism in our lives, many of which we don't even recognize. I have interacted with some professing believers who were truly in bondage to legalism. Enslaved by their list of rules, life for them is literally nothing by a long litany of do's and don'ts. They spend all their time applying the rules not only to themselves but to everyone around them. When I think of these people, the one all-encompassing adjective that always comes to mind is the word *joyless*. The Christian life is utterly without joy or peace or happiness. It is nothing but a duty, a grind, a drudgery. I have also observed that these individuals often have a very difficult time forgiving others; the people around them keep failing to live up to the standards that have been imposed, and the legalist can develop a heart that holds on to grievances. But whatever form legalism takes, it's a totally depressing way for a believer to live and never what the Lord intended for His children.

This is a humorous yet tragic poem that reveals the perspective of the legalist:

Believe as I believe—no more, no less;
That I am right (and no one else) confess.
Feel as I feel, think only as I think;
Eat what I eat, and drink what I drink.
Look as I look, do always as I do;
Then—and only then—I'll fellowship with you.[2]

## LIBERTY THAT LOVES

### *The Strong and the Weak*

The other side of this balance is the freedom that we have in Christ, something we are grateful for. But when it comes to Christian liberty, we must remember that our freedoms are accompanied by biblical guidelines. In Romans 14, we find the apostle Paul addressing a significant issue in the church at Rome—the presence of what he calls "strong" and "weak" believers. These two descriptions deal with an individual's ability to apply the doctrine of justification by faith to daily living. Those who are called the *strong in faith* are those who understand that once a person has been justified by faith, nothing can change that position. In contrast, the *weak in faith* are those who struggle to believe that they are completely accepted by God and thus they tend to create rules for themselves in an attempt to soothe their consciences. Every local church has the strong and weak brothers that Romans 14 talks about. Paul's greater point in the chapter is that we *must* be ruled by love when those brothers and sisters have different convictions. Also, we must be careful to remain humble and teachable before the Lord, making certain that our freedoms are true preference issues that are not prohibited in the Bible.

### *Handle with Care*

If you have a Christian liberty that you can enjoy with a clear conscience before the Lord, yet you know it might offend a brother or sister in Christ, what should you do? If you love them, there is really only one course to follow: enjoy your freedom humbly, wisely, and privately, thanking God that in His grace, He has chosen to allow His children certain pleasures in this world. What we cannot do is flaunt our personal liberties to the harm of others. It is truly sad how many do this very thing all over the various avenues of social media. In this current day when unity among believers is already so fragile, why would anyone want to unnecessarily offend their brothers and sisters by parading their particular liberties in front of those who may hold different convictions? What good purpose could that possibly serve? The truth is that it is *not* loving; it is actually quite selfish. We must always handle our freedoms carefully. In these situations involving different convictions, we would do well to heed Paul's heartfelt plea in Ephesians 4:

> I therefore, a prisoner for the Lord, urge you to walk in a manner worthy of the calling to which you have been called, with all humility and gentleness, with patience, bearing with one another in love, eager to maintain the unity of the Spirit in the bond of peace. (4:1-3)

### A Conscience Trained by the Word

Perhaps one more thought is in order here related to the personal preferences we may hold that differ from others. We should never encourage other believers to indulge in any behavior that would violate their consciences. To ignore one's conscience is a dangerous thing to do—it desensitizes a person to its voice and thus to the protective role it plays in their life. And this may lead to potentially participating in activities that can cause a wounded conscience to respond with deep feelings of guilt (Romans 14:13-23; 1 Corinthians 8:9-13). In contrast, a number of the New Testament writers comment on the value of a clear conscience (Acts 24:16; Romans 13:5; 1 Timothy 1:5,19; 3:9; 2 Timothy 1:3; Hebrews 13:18; 1 Peter 3:16). Of course, it is possible for Christians to have a conscience that is not trained properly by Scripture. This can result in the formation of unnecessary convictions and actions that are dictated by improper thinking. If we have people in our lives that we think are possibly holding an unbiblical conviction, we should both pray for them and encourage them to stay under sound teaching from God's Word. As they inform their consciences with Scripture and the indwelling Holy Spirit instructs and enlightens their minds, the hope (and strong probability) is that their convictions will gradually become more and more biblical.

## A WORD FOR PARENTS

As we close this chapter on maintaining a proper balance between self-denial and liberty, I want to relate this balance to the area of raising children. Our natural bent toward legalism and externalism has considerable implications for those of us who are parents. It's very tempting to pacify ourselves with our children's outward obedience and neglect crucial heart issues such as pride or selfishness or anger. When we fail to address these deeper issues, we are unintentionally setting our children up to be little Pharisees who are much more concerned with the outside than the inside. Then, as they grow up, especially in the teen years, the danger is that they can unfortunately become quite adept at hiding their true spiritual condition beneath a façade of external righteousness. The last thing we want to do is encourage hypocrisy in our children. Dealing with the heart from the very beginning and lovingly showing them their need for a Savior is wise parenting.

## *Don't Twist the Word*

Parents, always be honest with your children about the principles found in Scripture. Trust the truth we find there! Never twist the scriptures to make them say what you want them to say in a desperate attempt to control your children's behavior. Instead of teaching them to live only by your rules, teach your kids from a young age to turn to God's Word and seek the Lord's help in doing what is right. Obviously, the younger the child, the more they need structure and discipline with clear-cut rules and guidelines. "House rules" can be very helpful when dealing with young children. But as they grow up and eventually mature into young adults, the reliance on rules should diminish as we increasingly bring biblical insights to bear on concerns in their lives. They must learn to seek the Lord's guidance in making wise decisions on what they do and don't do. They need to think carefully about these important topics of self-denial and freedom and what it means for them personally. We need to encourage them to regularly ask themselves these questions: *What does God say in the Bible about this issue? What would the Lord have me do in this situation? What will enable me to show love to other people?* Do your utmost to help your children develop a proper fear of the Lord (Proverbs 1:7; 2:5-6; 3:7) so that they learn to run everything in their lives through the grid of God and His Word.

## *Trusting God for Our Children*

As we endeavor to faithfully shepherd our children, one of our most difficult tasks as parents is to learn to rest in God's sovereignty and trust the Holy Spirit to do His convicting, guiding work in their hearts. This can be quite challenging because too often, our default setting as parents is to rely solely on our own ability to control them. But simply insisting that they follow a long list of rules is the easy way out! You are not doing your children a favor by making them dependent on rules and regulations instead of diligently teaching them to apply God's Word to their lives. Parents have a huge responsibility here to pass *truth* on to our children. Sadly, too many times we see older kids reach young adulthood and walk away from the church, from everything they were taught growing up, maybe even from their faith altogether. Regrettably, they may never have thought through the hard questions from a scriptural viewpoint. They may never have grasped how helpful and intensely practical the Bible is in dealing with the challenges of everyday life (2 Peter 1:3). Tragically, they may never have learned how to connect the nuts and bolts of biblical truth to the temptations and pressures of this world (1 Corinthians 10:13). Then once they are free from all those rules, they plunge headlong into all the false promises and allurements of this world. Sometimes they come back. Sometimes they don't. For the parent who has literally poured their life into their child for many years, there is no greater heartbreak than this.

## *The Power of Prayer*

Parents, consider this reality: there will come a time in your children's lives when they are adults and you will basically have no control over them whatsoever. At this point, your primary ministry is prayer on their behalf (and perhaps giving them counsel if they ask for it.) Therefore, from their earliest days, develop a faithful practice of praying for your children and committing them to the Lord. Never stop praying, no matter how old they are. Pray that the Holy Spirit will do in their hearts what we are powerless to do. Model to them a parent who loves God and who believes in the power of intercessory prayer.

### Relationship, Not Just Rules

As mentioned in the previous chapter, despite our best intentions, all parents make mistakes. Because we are sinful human beings, there will be times when our choices and judgments are flawed. At these times, we must trust that a merciful Father knows our hearts and will somehow use our feeble efforts for good in our children's lives. Thankfully, though, there are some foundational commitments that will assist us greatly in our parenting. First, it's imperative that we treasure our children as precious, priceless gifts to us from the Lord (Psalm 127:3, NASB). Second, we must make it our goal to build the strongest relationship with them that we possibly can: we need to love them, discipline them, teach them, train them, listen to them, support them, do serious things with them, do fun things with them! Make as many memories with them as possible. Someday that relationship may carry you through some difficult times. If all you ever give your children is a list of rules to obey and you are not putting significant time and effort into building a strong, trusting relationship with them, you may unfortunately be laying the groundwork for a loss of fellowship with them, or even worse, for their rebellion down the road.

### The Power of Agape Love

Above all, make sure that your children know that you love them and that nothing they say or do will ever change that. *Nothing!* As they become adults, you may not agree with all their opinions or choices, and at times you may be compelled to speak hard truth to them. Yet they must be assured that these things have no bearing whatsoever on your unwavering love for them. You want the best for them. You are on their team and always will be! This is *agape* love, which is the kind of love that our Father has for us as His children. This is the love that takes no thought for self but is only concerned with the good of the Beloved. The Shulamite bride in Song of Solomon gives us some eloquent musings on the power of love, that "love is as strong as death...many waters cannot quench love, nor can the floods drown it" (8:6-7). These verses have been called the "1 Corinthians 13" of the Old Testament. This kind of unstoppable love will be a powerful force in your children's lives.

## THE EXTREMES

Let us look at the potential perils in this far-reaching area of self-denial and liberty. If you are too extreme on the side of *self-denial*, here are the dangers:

- Self-righteousness
- Legalism/works-righteousness
- An inability to enjoy Christian freedom

- Prideful judging and lack of love toward fellow
  believers

On the other hand, if you're unbalanced on the side of
*liberty*, here are the symptoms that may become evident:

- Sinfulness/worldliness
- License (disregard of God's moral code)
- Selfish flaunting of Christian liberty
- Prideful judging and lack of love toward fellow
  believers

Achieving balance in this vast area is a true challenge.
First, it is imperative that we come to a correct biblical
understanding of the gospel and what comprises true righteousness in our lives. We must never forget that good
works are the *result* of our salvation, not the means of it.
God's Word needs to be studied carefully to fully comprehend the priority of holy living and the devastating
effects of worldliness. Moreover, it is always beneficial to
solicit counsel from mature Christians who can help us as
we examine our lives. Finally, we must humbly seek the
Lord's wisdom and guidance in developing our personal
convictions and trust that He is also at work in the lives
of our fellow believers.

## *For Personal Reflection and Application*

### CHAPTER 3—SELF-DENIAL AND LIBERTY

1.  What did Jesus mean in Luke 9:23 when He said that His true disciple must deny himself and die to himself daily? (Also see 2 Corinthians 5:14-15.) What are the practical implications for our choices in life? What should it look like when "the love of Christ controls us"?

2.  Explain "legalism" ("works-righteousness") in your own words. How is this danger expressed vertically toward God? How is it expressed toward other people? By what external standards have you been tempted to judge others?

3.  What are some common "gray areas" where Christians have different preferences? What is the right response toward other believers who do not share the same conviction in a particular area? (Romans 14:3-4,13)

4.  What is the danger of misunderstanding or misusing your freedom in Christ? (Galatians 5:13)

5.  In 1 Corinthians 6:12, the apostle Paul said, "All things are lawful for me, but not all things are profitable" (NASB). How can the question, "Is it profitable?" help you make wise

decisions? What was Paul's concern in 1 Corinthians 9:27?

6.  When we love our fellow believers, we will choose to handle our freedoms carefully so as not to offend others or cause someone to stumble. What is the danger of tempting another believer to ignore their conscience? (1 Corinthians 8:9-12; Romans 14:13-15, 20-23)

# ENDNOTES

1   Piper, J. (2004). *When I Don't Desire God: How to Fight for Joy* (Wheaton, IL: Crossway Books), 85.

2   Swindoll, C. (1983). *Growing Strong in the Seasons of Life* (Grand Rapids, MI: Zondervan), 286.

*Good sense makes one slow to anger, and
it is his glory to overlook an offense.*
—Proverbs 19:11

*Be kind to one another, tenderhearted,
forgiving one another...*
—Ephesians 4:32

*...love covers a multitude of sins.*
—1 Peter 4:8

*"If your brother sins against you,
go and tell him his fault..."*
—Matthew 18:15

*"If your brother sins, rebuke him..."*
—Luke 17:3

*...you yourselves are full of goodness,
filled with all knowledge
and able also to admonish one another.*
—Romans 15:14 (NASB)

## Chapter 4
# PATIENCE AND CONFRONTATION

The Guadalupe River in Texas is a significant waterway, running for more than 200 miles as it winds its way from central Texas all the way down to the Gulf of Mexico. It has long been known as a popular vacation destination for canoeing, kayaking, rafting, fly-fishing, and a variety of other water sports. Long sections of the river are completely placid and peaceful, allowing you to drift quietly on an inner tube and basically do nothing for hours in the warm Texas sun. Yet there are other stretches where the river narrows and the sharp rocks underneath transform the deceptively calm stream into a churning cauldron of angry water! In those places, you cannot "do nothing" or you will quickly find yourself *in* the river instead of *on top* of it.

All along the river, specific entrance and exit points are clearly marked and strictly enforced. These points serve several purposes, not the least of which is to protect an unsuspecting person on an inner tube from unintentionally ending up on a section of the river known for its whitewater rapids. For the sake of public safety, a number of factors related to the river are continually monitored, especially during the rainy season when conditions can quickly change and the swift currents can become extremely dangerous.

While whitewater rafters relish the thrill of navigating the rapids, a vast number of other vacationers prefer to simply relax and quietly meander down the river on inner tubes or rubber rafts. Especially in the spring and summer, there can be hundreds of these on the river at any one time. Drifting along in an inner tube or raft is an easy endeavor, requiring no real skill whatsoever. Yet you still have to be prepared for the unexpected, as I learned the hard way.

Growing up in Texas, my husband and I had several opportunities to enjoy the Guadalupe through the years, and one particular visit stands out in our minds. We were on a church trip, and about ten of us were in a large raft, floating lazily and effortlessly down the river. Suddenly we became aware of people on the riverbank waving frantically and shouting at us while pointing downriver. Confused, we looked ahead but saw nothing. Unbeknownst to us, we had somehow missed a crucial juncture along the way, setting us on an irreversible course toward a five-foot drop over a concrete dam in the river! By the time we actually heard the roar of the water ahead, it was too late to do anything but make whatever emergency preparations we could. Springing into action, we huddled in the middle of the raft, getting down as low as possible while desperately holding onto our paddles and the safety ropes. As we went over the falls, the raft folded up like a pancake, throwing us all together into a jumbled mess of wet humanity!

Fortunately, no one was hurt or thrown overboard, and we all had a great laugh about it afterwards. But I've never forgotten how instantly our peaceful journey was transformed into an agitated burst of frenzied activity. Having virtually no warning, we did not have any choice at that point but to deal with our new situation as best we could. Simply allowing ourselves to be passively carried along as we had been was no longer an option.

We can find in this story a reflection of our lives in this world. There are times when we are enjoying the relatively quiet part of the river, drifting along with the status quo, patiently watching and waiting instead of taking action. Then suddenly a difficult situation or circumstance arises, and it becomes clear that doing nothing is no longer possible. But unlike the Guadalupe River, there are no clearly marked entrance and exit signs along the way that warn us of these difficult stretches in life. As in our experience that day on the river, more often than not, we're blindsided by the situation with very little warning of what lies ahead.

Sadly, not only can these challenging times involve our own sinfulness, they often can involve the faults and failings of others and the offenses that are committed against us. When do we choose to drift along and be patient, and when do we choose to act? When do we overlook, and when do we confront? These questions are at the heart of our next discussion and once again, this balance is intensely practical because it impacts many conversations and interactions that we have on a daily basis. In any given situation, we can frequently find ourselves trying to determine if we should lean toward *patience* or *confrontation*. Making a wise decision about *if* and *when* an issue should be directly dealt with requires much discernment and prayer.

## THE RIGHT THING AT THE RIGHT TIME

Let us define our terms so we appreciate their full significance. *Patience* is such a rich word. It carries the meaning of "longsuffering; forbearance under provocation or strain; the bearing of pains or trials calmly or without complaint; steadfastness despite opposition, difficulty, or adversity."[1] What wonderful qualities to strive for in our lives! On the other hand, *confrontation* means "to meet face to face; to deal with; to present to someone for acknowledgment; a technique in which one is forced to recognize one's shortcomings and their possible consequences."[2] Patience, therefore, can be expressed in the choice to wait and *not* confront or force an issue at a particular moment. To summarize this balance: there is a right time to overlook an offense and show mercy and grace to the other person, just as there is also a right time to take action and deal decisively with sin.

As we study our Lord's ministry here on earth, we see again that He is our example of perfect balance. Jesus Christ was a consistent proclaimer of unadulterated, overwhelming truth. He *is* the Truth; no one ever spoke like this Man (John 14:6; 7:46). He boldly confronted the Pharisees and religious hypocrites of His day with incredibly strong words of condemnation (Matthew 23:1-36; John 8:44). Yet no one has ever been as humble and kind and gracious as Jesus (Matthew 11:29). We think of His gentle interaction with the woman at the well (John 4:1-42). We see Him healing untold numbers of sick and suffering people throughout the Gospels. We marvel at His ongoing patience in countless instances with His own disciples (Matthew 20:28; Mark 9:33-37; 10:35-40; John 21:15-19). There are numerous scriptures that tell us of His great compassion (Matthew 9:36; 14:14; 15:32; Mark 6:34; 8:2; Luke 7:13). John 1:14 says He was "full of grace and truth," and we see that balance demonstrated over and over again in His ministry.

## WHAT DOES IT MEAN TO COVER SIN?

Both the Old and New Testaments contain significant verses that will aid us in our understanding of covering sin. One well-known passage that comes to mind is Psalm 32:1. John MacArthur comments on this verse and the meaning of the word *cover*:

> Speaking of God's forgiveness, Psalm 32:1 equates the concepts of forgiveness and the covering of sin: "How blessed is he whose transgression is forgiven, whose sin in covered!" This is a Hebrew parallelism, employing two different expressions to designate the same concept. To cover someone else's sin is the very essence of forgiveness.[3]

We see *cover* used again in Psalm 85:2. The psalmist here is praising God because "You forgave the iniquity of your people; you covered all their sin." Proverbs also employs this term when it tells us: "Hatred stirs up strife, but love covers all transgressions" (Proverbs 10:12, NASB). The commentators Keil and Delitzsch provide insight on this verse:

> [L]ove covers not merely little errors, but also greater sins of every kind...by pardoning them, concealing them, excusing them, if possible, with mitigating circumstances, or restraining them before they are executed. All this lies in the covering.[4]

In the Old Testament, therefore, covering is clearly linked with the attitude of forgiveness. The further point being made in Proverbs 10:12 is that the one who covers also avoids "stirring up" sins or broadcasting them to others but instead suffers silently and bears them.[5]

Moving on to the New Testament, we find a comparable thought from the apostle Peter in his first epistle: "Above all, keep loving one another earnestly, since love covers a multitude of sins" (1 Peter 4:8). Several commentators believe that this verse is not a direct quote of Proverbs 10:12, although it is very similar. Instead, the thought is that Peter is merely referring to a common saying that was based on the scripture in Proverbs.[6] Regardless of the connection, and though there are differing interpretations of the exact meaning, this verse in 1 Peter is applicable to our discussion:

> It is self-evident that genuine love inherently tends to forgive the offenses of others (cf. Proverbs 10:12). But commentators differ on how to interpret the expression "love covers a multitude of sins." Some

say it refers to God's love covering sins, whereas others say it describes believers who are lovingly overlooking each other's transgressions. Since the text offers no explanation, it seems best to understand the phrase here as a general axiom. Whether from God or man, love covers sin.[7]

It is important to recognize that we can "cover" sins in two ways: either by confronting the other person directly or by choosing to overlook. Either way we are dealing with it, and as we will see, examples of both are given to us in Scripture. No matter which "covering" path we choose in a certain set of circumstances, the goal is always the same: to grant forgiveness and seek reconciliation. Both responses, overlooking or confronting, are driven by love and a concern for the supreme good of the other person. Once again, we must pray for wisdom to discern which response is in their best interest in any specific situation.

## A TIME TO OVERLOOK

Several passages in the Bible indicate there are times when we are allowed to overlook a sin that has been committed against us. Proverbs 19:11 states: "Good sense makes one slow to anger, and it is his glory to overlook an offense." We are further told: "He who covers a transgression seeks love" (Proverbs 17:9, NKJV). We have already mentioned 1 Peter 4:8. In the MacArthur Study Bible, the note on this verse in 1 Peter comments that "a Christian should overlook sins against him if possible, and always be ready to forgive insults and unkindnesses."[8] From Romans 3:23, it is painfully clear that we are *all* sinners and we *all* fall short at times. So especially when the offense is small or unintentional, our default setting should always be to overlook and forgive. Consider what 1 Corinthians 13 says about *agape* love:

> Love is patient and kind...it is not arrogant or rude. It does not insist on its own way; it is not irritable or resentful...Love bears all things, believes all things, hopes all things, endures all things. (13:4-5,7)

One meaningful way to show love to fellow believers is by choosing to not constantly confront them on the slightest infractions. If a formal meeting was required in every instance of a believer's failure, there would never be time for anything else in church life! We would spend the bulk of our days doing nothing but dealing with and resolving conflicts between Christians. Ephesians 4 urges us to bear with one another and do our utmost to maintain unity and peace in our interpersonal relationships "with all humility and gentleness, with patience, bearing with one another in love, eager to maintain the unity of the Spirit in the bond of peace" (4:2-3).

### What Is Our Default Setting?

As Christians, we should have a reputation for being humble, gracious people who patiently endure the failings and shortcomings of others. We have received forgiveness from Christ; our first response to an offense should therefore be forgiveness, not irritation or condemnation. Romans 2:4 reminds us that "God's kindness is meant to lead us to repentance." So who is to say that He will not use *our* kindness the same way in another believer's life? It should therefore be our goal to become this type of longsuffering person. A verse in Psalm 119 gives us one of the secrets to maintaining a tranquil and forbearing spirit: "Great peace have those who love your law; nothing can make them stumble" (119:165). The *more* we fill up our minds and hearts with the Word of God, the *less* we will be disturbed or offended by the actions of the people around us.

### The Common Thread

Something else that will assist us in our pursuit of patience is to be very conscious of our own sinfulness and weaknesses. This will go a long way in helping us empathize with the shortcomings of others. How can we be harsh and irritable with others when we are so painfully aware of our own inconsistencies? My father was a very forgiving man who never held a grudge. In my entire life, I never heard him raise his voice; I never saw him lose his temper. He had a favorite saying that I heard many times as I was growing up: "I don't understand the things *I* do, much less understand the things that *other* people do!" It was this perspective that enabled him to be extraordinarily patient with all those around him. We all say and do things at times that are unintentional or thoughtless, and we regret them later. Often, in hindsight, we don't even understand why we did it. My father was infinitely gracious to people because he understood that we are all alike: we are *all* sinners, we *all* make mistakes. It should always be our goal to be as longsuffering with others as we hope they will be with us.

## A TIME TO CONFRONT

We have thus seen that there are times when we should overlook and forgive offenses without ever bringing it up to the other person. There are several scriptures, however, that tell us we absolutely have a responsibility to confront sin. Jesus' words in Luke 17:3 are in the form of a direct command: "If your brother sins, rebuke him." We find a similar thought in Matthew 18: "If your brother sins against you, go and tell him his fault, between you and him alone" (18:15). And in Romans 15:14, the apostle Paul also acknowledges that Christians are at times "to admonish one another." A familiar verse in Galatians teaches that "if anyone is caught in any transgression, you who are spiritual should restore him in a spirit of gentleness" (6:1). What makes this verse so interesting is that while it is obviously saying that the transgression should be dealt with, Paul chose to use the word *restore* instead of the word *confront*. This is a wonderful and needed reminder that the purpose of all confrontation is to restore, not to attack or condemn. This thought is further reinforced by Paul's encouragement to do it "in a spirit of gentleness."

*Compassion, Not Condemnation*

Proverbs 28:23 is another intriguing verse related to this topic: "Whoever rebukes a man will afterward find more favor than he who flatters with his tongue." This scripture is making the crucial point that "rebuke" is more profitable in the long term than "flattering" (i.e., refusing to deliver a needed correction). A key word in this verse is *afterward*. Confrontation is often uncomfortable or painful in the short term, yet after some time has passed, the hope is that the one who was spoken to will realize it was ultimately for his good. Paul reinforces this point in 2 Corinthians 7:8-9 where he rejoiced that his strong words in a letter had eventually brought the Corinthians to godly grief and sorrow over their sin.

In Psalm 51, that great psalm of repentance, David cries out, "Restore to me the joy of your salvation" (51:12). He had not lost his salvation, but he had lost the *joy* of it. This is a potent reminder that sin is a terrible destroyer. It destroys joy; it destroys fellowship; it destroys relationships. The cost is great. So while we know there are risks to confronting sin, many times the greater risk is to *not* confront it.

Never forget that our goal is always restoration and reconciliation. Always! In Matthew 18, our Lord clearly affirms that the purpose of confrontation is to win our brother, not to harm him:

> If your brother sins, go and show him his fault in private; if he listens to you, you have won your brother. (18:15, NASB)

Our motive is never to punish or alienate another believer. In contrast, the objective is to gently bring the sinning brother back into fellowship with his Lord and with others in the body of Christ.

### Watch Out for Preferences

Another key point here is that confrontation should be reserved for legitimate instances of sin or offensive behavior. We find a number of passages in the Bible that warn against clearly defined sins of the heart and body, and these must be taken seriously (Mark 7:21-23; Romans 13:13; 1 Corinthians 6:9-10; Galatians 5:19-21; Ephesians 4:29-31; 5:3-5; Colossians 3:5-8; 2 Timothy 3:2-5). We do, however, need to be careful that we actually have solid scriptural support before we ever address sin concerns with another believer. There is an important reminder in Proverbs to make sure we have all the facts before dealing with an offense: "If one gives an answer before he hears, it is his folly and shame" (18:13). Also remember that we do not confront for differing opinions on non-biblical issues, as previously discussed in chapter 3. In these situations, we can certainly dialogue about our diverse perspectives, but it's imperative that we learn to respect the convictions and preferences of those who do not think exactly as we do. Finally, we must understand that while there are certainly minor or unintentional offenses that can sometimes be overlooked, these too may eventually call for confrontation if they are part of a troubling and persistent pattern.

### Remove Those Logs!

Finally, if we have carefully determined that an offense needs to be addressed, it is essential that we look to ourselves first. We must humbly inspect our own lives, making certain there are no "logs" that need to be removed:

> Why do you see the speck that is in your brother's eye, but do not notice the log that is in your own eye? Or how can you say to your brother, "Let me take the speck out of your eye," when there is the

log in your own eye? You hypocrite, first take the log out of your own eye, and then you will see clearly to take the speck out of your brother's eye. (Matthew 7:3-5)

Our self-examination should also include an evaluation of our motives to make certain they are not selfish. We need to guard against confronting out of personal irritation or annoyance. Instead, what should drive us is love for Christ and a genuine love and concern for our brother or sister. The importance of this cannot be overstated: if you want to "win" your brother, you must cultivate the right heart attitude. Above all, we pray for the Lord's wisdom and ask Him to guide us every step along the way in this process.

### The Biblical Process of Confrontation

Once we have concluded that a confrontation is necessary, we go in the spirit of Galatians 6:1, approaching our brother or sister in Christ humbly, privately, and prayerfully. We ask appropriate questions that will ensure we are evaluating the situation correctly (Proverbs 18:13). We gently bring our concerns to him or her, perhaps helping them see how their sin dishonors the Lord and can potentially bring about serious consequences in their lives and the lives of others. We then pray with them and for them and graciously call them to repentance.

Hopefully, your fellow believer will receive your loving correction and acknowledge their offense. If they resist, however, we are then to follow the principles of Matthew 18, bringing two or three others with us to verify information and make another humble appeal. If the offender still refuses to listen, church leadership must move on to the step of bringing the matter before the entire body. In the cases where there is still no response, Matthew 18 instructs us to remove the unrepentant sinner from the church as we continue to pray for a contrite heart and sorrow over their sin. Once more, it is critical to understand that the steps of church discipline found in Matthew 18 are intended to be redemptive, not punitive. The goal, along with the purity of the church, is always full restoration of the individual.

### Receiving Correction from Others

There is also a word here for us if it should ever happen that *we* are the ones being corrected. Proverbs 27:17 tells us, "Iron sharpens iron, and one man sharpens another." We must be humble enough to be sharpened! A man or woman who is painfully aware of their own sinfulness is a teachable person. If confronted, they will not be defensive or retaliate but will honestly examine themselves to see if they are truly at fault. The book of Proverbs describes this kind of person:

> Whoever heeds instruction is on the path to life, but he who rejects reproof leads others astray. (10:17)

> Do not reprove a scoffer, or he will hate you; reprove a wise man, and he will love you. (9:8)

> The ear that listens to life-giving reproof will dwell among the wise. (15:31)

One of the chief characteristics of a wise man is his humility, and one of the most reliable marks of humility is teachability. A teachable man knows how to receive correction and learns from it, and in the end, it will only serve to make him wiser (Prov. 9:9). In contrast, a proud man is called a "scoffer" and is unteachable. We must always be on guard against this attitude in our lives.

## WHAT ABOUT UNBELIEVERS?

In this discussion, we have been mainly focusing on our interactions with other believers. Yet there may be times when we are called upon to speak boldly to those who do not belong to Christ. We find a compelling passage in the book of James that reminds us of the importance of caring enough to confront the unbelievers in our lives, and once again we see the significant concept of sins being covered.

My brothers, if anyone among you wanders from the truth and someone brings him back, let him know that whoever brings back a sinner from his wandering will save his soul from death and will cover a multitude of sins. (James 5:19-20)

While most of James' epistle is written to Jewish Christians, here in the last chapter he turns his attention to the unregenerate and concludes with these sobering verses. The context here is that of an individual "among you" who has at least outwardly identified with the church but has "wandered from the truth" and is in desperate need of being brought back. Daniel Burdick comments on this passage:

Since scripture teaches that once a person is regenerated he can never be lost, it may be assumed that this hypothetical wanderer is not a genuine believer. He would be one who had been among the believers and had a profession of faith, but his profession had been superficial. To bring him to genuine faith in the truth is to save his soul from eternal death. The result of bringing the wanderer back is that "many sins" will be covered.[9]

## *The Ministry of Reconciliation*

An astounding thought in all of this is that God allows us to have a part in it! Not only do we see this in James 5, we are also told in 2 Corinthians 5:18-20 that God has given us "the ministry of reconciliation." Concerning these opportunities for evangelism, we are reminded by MacArthur:

God has granted to all believers the ministry of reconciling wandering souls to Himself. When the evidence indicates a professed believer's faith is not real, true Christians, knowing the terrible threat of eternal death that person faces, must make it their goal to turn him back from his sin to genuine saving faith in God.[10]

And yet we must never forget that salvation is all of God! Commenting on these verses in James 5, R. Kent Hughes says, "What a blessed feat is accomplished when a sinner is turned away from his error. God alone does this. But he does use human instruments who love him and who love people."[11] Kistemaker also emphasizes this thought: "Salvation, then, is and remains God's work. We are only fellow workers for God."[12]

What a humbling thought to know that our loving reproof, our willingness to give a warning, might possibly be used in some small way by God to "bring back a sinner" from his wandering and save him from the consequences of his sin. Sin is deadly and we must always be concerned for an individual's spiritual well-being.

Just keep this vital point in mind when in the position of confronting an unbeliever: an unregenerate person has no real ability to conquer sin without the power of the indwelling Holy Spirit. When we encounter the sin of an unbeliever, therefore, we are calling them to believe, repent and surrender to the Lordship of Jesus Christ, while praying for the Spirit to do the saving work that only He can do.

## THE QUESTIONS TO ASK

### The Big Picture

In summary, when faced with issues of sin in another believer's life, we can choose to overlook or we can confront. Here are some basic questions to consider that will help us make the right choice. Is this a single instance of failure, or is this a pattern in their lives? Was it deliberate or unintentional? Are they repentant and willing to confess their offense? Are they taking responsibility for their own actions or do they frequently lay the blame on others? The answers to these questions will help us act wisely.

## *The Effect on Others*

Some additional questions need to be asked that relate specifically to the area of interpersonal relationships. How is the individual being personally harmed by their sin, and what effect is it having on the other people in their lives? One of the sad realities about sin is that it never affects only the sinner but can also carry weighty implications for those closest to him. Although we understand that the offense is first and foremost against a holy God (Psalm 51:4), the damage done to other people can be significant. While there are differing viewpoints on the exact connotation of the terms "forgiveness" and "reconciliation" and how they are fleshed out practically in our lives,[13] these two concepts are essential goals if we are to maintain peace in our relationships. When a believer sinfully refuses to forgive and pursue reconciliation with another person, not only are their human relationships impacted but infinitely more significant, their relationship with the Lord is severely affected (Psalm 66:18; Proverbs 28:9). In Matthew 5:23-24, we are reminded of the necessity of addressing and repairing broken relationships before we can properly worship God with a clear conscience.

Furthermore, Scripture instructs us that in these breaches of relationship, *both* individuals have a responsibility to seek the restoration of peace:

> If you are the offended party, Luke 17:3 applies: "If your brother sins, rebuke him." You are the one who must go to him. If you are the offender,

Matthew 5:23-24 applies: "If...you are presenting your offering at the altar, and there remember that your brother has something against you, leave your offering there before the altar, and go your way; first be reconciled to your brother."[14]

Romans 12:18 acknowledges that, unfortunately, reconciliation with another individual may not always be attainable: "If possible, so far as it depends on you, live peaceably with all." Simply put, we are to do all that is within our power to be at peace with others.

### The Reflection on Christ and the Church

Returning to our discussion of when to overlook and when to confront, other questions dealing with doctrine and the Church are equally important. Is the offender misrepresenting or dishonoring the name of Christ? Is orthodox teaching being opposed? In the letter to Titus, we are clearly instructed to rebuke those who contradict sound doctrine (1:9). Is this individual denying the truth or the implications of the gospel? The book of Galatians gives an honest account of how Paul publicly rebuked Peter due to his hypocrisy in the presence of the Gentile believers. In the second chapter, Paul explains that the correction was necessary because Peter's conduct was "not in step with the gospel" (2:14). Finally, is this a scandalous sin (1 Corinthians 5:1-5) that damages the testimony of the Church? Answering all these questions will be helpful in determining what our response should be.

## THE WRONG KIND OF FEAR

What then are the evidences in our lives when we go to the extreme on either side of this balance? When we are excessive on the side of patience, we can be guilty of refusing to speak necessary truth to others and never dealing with an offense that needs to be confronted. What this generally reveals is what the Bible calls "fear of man." We find this sin addressed in Proverbs 29:25: "The fear of man lays a snare, but whoever trusts in the LORD is safe." Fear of man is basically caring more about what *people* think of us than what *God* thinks of us. We are afraid of what may happen to our reputation with other people; we might be labeled legalistic or judgmental. We are afraid of offending others and damaging or losing a relationship. We can be anxious about any number of consequences that may result from speaking hard but necessary truth to another individual. The fear of man can thus reveal a lack of love for other people since true love will always do what is best for others, no matter what it may cost us personally. Their well-being is our highest priority even if it requires sacrifice on our part.

*True Love*

Remember this: there are instances when the most loving thing you can do, the highest pinnacle of love, is to tell someone the truth. Ephesians 4:25 gives us this admonition: "Therefore, having put away falsehood, let each one of you speak the truth with his neighbor, for we are members one of another." It is wrong to withhold the truth from someone when they desperately need to hear it!

When their sin is dishonoring the Lord, or hurting them personally and everyone around them, it is indefensible to stay quiet. Unchecked sin will eventually lead to spiritual shipwreck. If we love them, how can we stand by and say nothing?

## CAUSTIC CONFRONTATION

On the other hand, we know it is also possible to err on the side of confrontation. If your focus seems to always be on speaking the truth (with an attitude untempered by grace) and confronting every fault and failure that you come across, this can possibly reveal a prideful, judgmental heart. Unfortunately, there are Christians who appear to have the mistaken notion that there is a spiritual gift called "confrontation" and their "ministry" is to confront everyone in the church body on their sin, large or small! If you have allowed yourself to develop this type of ungracious, overly critical spirit, you will alienate your sisters and brothers in Christ and may have great difficulty building relationships within the church body. You do not want people to run the other way when they see you coming! This type of condemning spirit is an especially serious problem if it is happening regularly in a marriage and can potentially be disastrous for the relationship.

There are other believers who, while not overtly confrontive, may still lack grace and kindness in many of their dealings with others and thus can leave a long trail of misunderstandings and hurt feelings behind them. If you are constantly having to circle back and do damage control with other people (both believers and unbelievers), you may need to take a long, hard look at how you interact with others. Key factors to examine would include not only your actual words but also your voice tone and volume. Another consideration would be your nonverbal communication, such as eye contact, facial expressions, and physical gestures. Are these things drawing people to you or driving them away?

## THE EXTREMES

To summarize, what are the common symptoms we may see if we are struggling with the balance between patience and confrontation? What should we look for? If you never confront sin and are excessive in your emphasis on *patience*, this may reveal the following issues:

- Fear of man
- Fear of losing reputation or relationships
- Lack of sacrificial love for others

If you are out of balance on the side of *confrontation*, these characteristics may begin to surface in your life:

- Pride/judgmentalism
- A critical, ungracious spirit
- Difficulty in building and maintaining relationships

Keep this principle in mind: when it comes to dealing with our brothers and sisters in Christ, always be much more concerned with your *own* sin than with the sins of everyone else. That will protect you and serve you well as you seek to balance patience with confrontation. Never confront others unless you are first dealing with your own shortcomings. Be ready to forgive any and all wrongs done to you (Psalm 86:5). Overlook whatever sins you legitimately can and deal courageously and lovingly with the ones you cannot.

## *For Personal Reflection and Application*

### CHAPTER 4—PATIENCE AND CONFRONTATION

1.  When is it appropriate to overlook another believer's sin? (Proverbs 19:11; Ephesians 4:32) What factors should we consider? Does this mean we are condoning sin?

2.  Name possible factors that can cause reluctance to address sin in relationships. (Proverbs 29:25)

3.  What did Jesus teach about forgiving the sins of others? (Matthew 18:21-22)

4.  How do Proverbs 27:5-6 and 28:23 portray the rebuke of a brother or sister in Christ? When we confront sin, what should our motive be?

5.  In Romans 15:14, what does Paul say qualifies one believer to admonish another? What is an essential prerequisite to confrontation? (Matthew 7:3-5)

6.  What are the warnings given to the person who is compelled to confront another believer? (Galatians 6:1-2) What is the goal of all reproof?

# ENDNOTES

1   Merriam-Webster.com. (2019). "patient." *Merriam-Webster. com.* https://www.merriam-webster.com. Accessed September 30, 2019.

2   Dictionary.com (2019). "confrontation." *Dictionary.com* based on the *Random House Unabridged Dictionary.* 2019.

3   MacArthur, J. (1998). *The Freedom and Power of Forgiveness* (Wheaton, IL: Crossway), 121.

4   Keil, C. F., and Delitzch, F. (2006). *Commentary on the Old Testament, Vol. 6* (Peabody, MA: Hendrickson Publishers, Inc.), 181.

5   Blum, E. A. (1981). *Expositor's Bible Commentary, Vol. 12* (Grand Rapids, MI: Zondervan), 246.

6   Hiebert, D. E. (1997). *1 Peter* (Winona Lake, IN: BMH Books), 273. James uses virtually the same words in James 5:20, leading scholars to assume that this proverb was probably circulated in the Jewish-Christian community of that day [Kistemaker, S. J. (1995). *New Testament Commentary* (Grand Rapids, MI: Baker Books), 167.]

7   MacArthur, J. (2004). *The MacArthur New Testament Commentary, 1 Peter* (Chicago, IL: Moody Press), 241.

8   MacArthur, J. (2006). *The MacArthur Study Bible* (Nashville, TN: Thomas Nelson), 1916.

9   Burdick, D. W. (1981). *Expositor's Bible Commentary, Vol. 12* (Grand Rapids, MI: Zondervan), 205.

10  MacArthur, J. *The Freedom and Power of Forgiveness,* 290.

11  Hughes, R. K. (1991). *James: Faith That Works* (Wheaton, IL: Crossway Books), 277.

12  Kistemaker, S. J. (1995). *New Testament Commentary: Exposition of James, Epistles of John, Peter, and Jude* (Grand Rapids, MI: Baker Books), 184.

13  For a fuller discussion of the meaning and implication of these words, see John MacArthur, "Just as God Has Forgiven You" in *The Freedom and Power of Forgiveness*, Chapter 6.

14  Ibid., 132.

*And God saw everything that he had made, and behold, it was very good.*
—Genesis 1:31

*Know well the condition of your flocks, and give attention to your herds...*
—Proverbs 27:23

*She looks well to the ways of her household and does not eat the bread of idleness.*
—Proverbs 31:27

*"And if I go and prepare a place for you, I will come again and will take you to myself..."*
—John 14:3

*Set your minds on things that are above...*
—Colossians 3:2

*...our citizenship is in heaven...*
—Philippians 3:20

## Chapter 5
# TEMPORAL AND ETERNAL

We all understand the concept of *quality* when it comes to the material things of this world. Items that are well-designed and well-made can be expected to last much longer than those that are not. A pair of shoes made of the highest quality leather will be wearable long after a pair of cheap sandals have completely worn out. Also, higher quality goods are usually more expensive than products made out of inferior materials, hence the saying "you get what you pay for" is a fairly accurate truism. It doesn't really matter what we're talking about. Whether we are referring to clothes or shoes or furniture or automobiles or houses, the principle still holds true. Some things are simply more valuable than others.

When it comes to this area of value and quality, we can also be deceived and tricked as to the true nature of an item. There is real gold, and there is iron pyrite, commonly called "fool's gold." There is real money, and there is counterfeit money. There is genuine leather, and there is imitation leather. Throughout the centuries, many masterpieces of art have been copied by forgers and successfully passed off as originals. In all these cases, the fake can look identical to the real thing, to the extent that only experts can determine the difference. And the list goes on and on: phony imitations of designer clothes, watches, handbags, sunglasses and countless other consumer products. There is no shortage of items in this world that claim to be valuable when, in actuality, they are merely fraudulent copies and relatively worthless.

Yet no matter whether something is of high quality or low, expensive or inexpensive, genuine or fake, all material items share one thing in common: they are part of this earthly realm and will someday cease to exist. Another contrast, however, is infinitely greater than the simple distinction between something that has worth and something that does not, and that is the incalculable disparity in value between everything that is part of this *temporal* world and that which belongs to another realm altogether, the realm of the *eternal*. The need to maintain a proper balance between the temporal and the eternal is something we face on a regular basis. This could also be described as the tension between the earthly and the heavenly. Virtually everything in our lives falls into one of these two categories.

## A TALE OF TWO KINGDOMS

*Temporal* is defined as "of or relating to time; pertaining to or concerned with the present life or this world; worldly."[1] All that comprises our earthly existence would be rightly listed here: our relationships, our vocations, our abilities and talents, our hobbies and interests, our responsibilities and obligations as citizens of this world. Temporal also includes the vast number of things that we apprehend with our five senses. Everything that we experience in this world belongs to the limited domain of the temporal.

In contrast, the *eternal* is an altogether different realm, completely unhindered by the constraints of time. It is the realm of the kingdom of God. The eternal encompasses all that we cannot experience through our physical senses in the usual way that we interact with the material things of this world. We cannot see our faith, although oftentimes we may see the practical outworking of it. We cannot physically touch God, although we see the assurance of His existence everywhere we look. Our faith in God, our relationship with Him, and our entire spiritual life all rest naturally and securely in the arms of the eternal. This word *eternal* is quite comfortable to us as believers because the definition we find in the dictionary echoes so many familiar words and concepts from Scripture: "without beginning or end; lasting forever; always existing; ceaseless; endless; enduring; immutable."[2] Everything related to our faith is rooted in the monumental truth that God and His Word are not temporal but eternal.

### *The Seen and the Unseen*
The Bible has its own poetic way of describing the difference between these two concepts, frequently utilizing the motif of the "seen" and the "unseen." Probably the clearest expression of this is found in 2 Corinthians 4:17-18 where the apostle Paul is addressing the issue of suffering:

For momentary, light affliction is producing for us an eternal weight of glory far beyond all comparison, while we look not at the things which are seen, but at the things which are not seen; for the things which are seen are temporal, but the things which are not seen are eternal. (NASB)

In this verse Paul is unequivocally stating that whatever we see is only temporary; the things that truly matter, the eternal things, are paradoxically the very things that we cannot see with our physical eyes.

This theme of the *seen* and the *unseen* appears a number of times in the New Testament. Hebrews 11 is a classic illustration. This chapter, commonly called the "Hall of Faith," lists several Bible figures who demonstrated faith in God by their belief and obedience. "Seeing the unseen" is always linked to faith and that reality is clearly illustrated in this chapter. It starts off with this declaration: "Faith is the assurance of things hoped for, the conviction of things not seen" (11:1). Then in verse 7, we are told: "By faith Noah, being warned by God concerning events as yet unseen, in reverent fear constructed an ark by faith...by this he...became an heir of the righteousness that comes by faith." Continuing on, the writer in verses 13 through 16 and also in verse 39 reminds us that these saints of old never received in their lifetimes what was promised to them. They well understood that this temporal world was not their home; they knew this was not all there was. Instead, they were seeking a better country—a *heavenly* country. Verse 13 explains that because they were "strangers and exiles on the earth," they "died in faith, without receiving the promises, but having seen them and having welcomed them from a distance." In other words, they actually saw with *spiritual* eyes what they could not see with physical ones. The last reference in Hebrews 11 to this supernatural sight is in connection to Moses in verse 27: "By faith he left Egypt, not fearing the wrath of the king; for he endured, as seeing Him who is unseen."

We also find this motif depicted elsewhere in Scripture. In Job 19:25-27, we see Job beginning to lift the eyes of his heart heavenward as he talks about his belief in the resurrection and his yearning to see his Redeemer. As we continue to make our way through the book, we finally come to Chapter 42, where Job gives this amazing testimony to the profitable result of all his unspeakable suffering:

> I had heard of you by the hearing of the ear, but now my eye sees you; therefore I despise myself, and repent in dust and ashes. (42:5-6)

Job's trials enabled him to know and understand the Lord—and himself—in a much deeper way. In other words, he had *seen* the character and purposes of God as he had never been able to before. This type of sight is truly supernatural and can only be granted to us by our Heavenly Father.

### The Cost of Seeing

Another illustration of seeing the unseen is found in the account of the death of Stephen, who was one of the seven men of integrity chosen by the early church. The Bible tells us in the book of Acts that he was "a man full of faith and of the Holy Spirit" and those who opposed him "could not withstand the wisdom and the Spirit with which he was speaking" (6:5,10). False witnesses were enlisted to accuse Stephen and he was brought before the Sanhedrin, where he gave a masterful analysis of Israel's history and then boldly proclaimed the gospel to them (6:11-7:50). As Stephen concluded his message, he accused them of being betrayers and murderers who had killed the Righteous One, just like their fathers who had killed the prophets, and this infuriated them (6:51-54). But the final straw was his passionate declaration in verse 55 that he was seeing the unseen:

> But he, full of the Holy Spirit, gazed into heaven and saw the glory of God, and Jesus standing at the right hand of God. And he said, "Behold, I see the heavens opened, and the Son of Man standing at the right hand of God." (7:55-56)

The Pharisees, because of their stubborn unbelief, were "blind leaders of the blind" (Matthew 15:14, NKJV), and they had no spiritual sight; they had no ability to see what Stephen was seeing. His words utterly enraged them. What he said was true, but the Pharisees viewed it as blasphemy. The angry mob then dragged him out of the city, where he was stoned to death as he prayed with compassion for his murderers just as Jesus had done on the cross. That day, as a result of his bold defense of the gospel and his testimony of what he *saw*, Stephen entered the annals of history as the very first Christian to be martyred for his faith.

## The Need to See

We must understand that as God's children, indwelt by the Holy Spirit, we have been given a precious gift: the gift of spiritual eyes that can see the unseen. And yet as human beings with a physical body, that is not our natural inclination. We desperately desire the gratification of seeing and touching with our physical senses. There is an example of this in the narrative of John 20:24-29. After the resurrection, when Jesus came and made His first appearance to His disciples, Thomas, one of the twelve, was not present. When the other disciples told him they had seen the risen Lord, this was Thomas's reply in verse 25: "But he said to them, 'Unless I see in his hands the mark of the nails, and place my finger into the mark of the nails, and place my hand into his side, I will never believe.'"

Thomas is a perfect illustration of our human need to physically see and touch. Eight days later, the Lord appeared again to His disciples, and this time Thomas was with them. Jesus did not rebuke him for his unbelief but graciously invited Thomas to look at the nail prints in His hands and touch His side, evoking from Thomas the heartfelt cry of "My Lord and my God!" in verse 28. What was Jesus' response in verse 29? "Have you believed because you have seen me? Blessed are those who have not seen and yet have believed."

What an encouragement to know that the Lord Himself pronounced a blessing on all of us who would believe without seeing in the many centuries that have passed since His resurrection. Moreover, what a joy it is to have the assurance that someday we *will* see Him! The book of 1 John tells us that when He appears, we shall be like

Him, and best of all, "we shall see Him as He is" (3:2). What an unspeakably glorious day that will be, to finally see the face of the Savior we have loved for so long! Who can even imagine what that will be like?

## *Hoping for What We Do Not See*

Until that future day, however, we remain children of the *unseen*. We are those who "walk by faith, not by sight" (2 Corinthians 5:7). We live in the encouraging reality of what theologians have called the *already but not yet*. Moreover, as we make our pilgrimage through this temporal life, hope in the Lord's return and our eternity in heaven is a fundamental part of our faith. Romans 8:24-25 explains why hope is linked so closely with faith: "Now hope that is seen is not hope. For who hopes for what he sees? But if we hope for what we *do not see*, we wait for it with patience."

Because we are strangers and exiles in this world, as Hebrews 11 tells us, and because of all the things that are still unseen, hope is essential for the Christian. Also, we must remember that the hope spoken of in Scripture is completely different from the hope that the world offers, which is often fraught with uncertainty and doubt. But *biblical* hope is rooted in the character of an unchanging, trustworthy God. In addition, the apostle Peter explains in his first epistle that because we are secure in Christ and have obtained the salvation of our souls, the "not seeing" does not diminish our love for our Savior: it simply makes us yearn more for the day when our faith will become sight.

Though you have not seen him, you love him. Though you do not now see him, you believe in him and rejoice with joy that is inexpressible and filled with glory, obtaining the outcome of your faith, the salvation of your soul. (1 Peter 1:8-9)

Elisabeth Elliot, in *Suffering is Never for Nothing,* alludes to this mystery of the seen and the unseen, the visible and the invisible:

We're talking about two different levels on which things are to be understood. And again and again in the Scriptures we have what seem to be complete paradoxes because we're talking about two different kingdoms. We're talking about this visible world and an invisible Kingdom on which the facts of this world are interpreted...Does it make any sense at all? Not unless you see that there are two kingdoms: the kingdom of this world, and the kingdom of an invisible world.[3]

## OVERLAPPING WORLDS

Before we continue, it's necessary to note that for a few things in this world, there is actually overlap between the temporal and the eternal. Some things legitimately fall under both categories and possess the characteristics of both. They currently exist on this earth, yet they will not come to an end when the earth does. God's Word would be one example of this. In this world, our written Bibles actually exist in a physical form. We can hold them in our hands and read the inspired words that are printed on pieces of paper. Furthermore, because our physical Bibles are part of a material world, they can actually be damaged or lost or even destroyed. We know, however, that the Word of God in its essence is eternal and will *never* be destroyed! Isaiah tells us it will stand forever (Isaiah 40:8). In Mark 13:31, Jesus reassures us that even though heaven and earth would pass away, His words (which were also physically heard by many during His earthly ministry) are eternal and will endure forever.

In a similar way, human beings, because they are created in the image of God, also bear the distinct imprint of both the temporal and the eternal. We find this monumental verse in the creation account of Genesis 1: "So God created man in his own image, in the image of God he created him; male and female he created them" (1:27). And because we alone are His image-bearers, He has made us eternal beings who are utterly unique, unlike anything else ever created. In addition, Ecclesiastes 3:11 tells us that God "put eternity into man's heart" and this underscores why we have such a deep longing in our souls for eternal things. What it means to be made in the image of our Creator is such a profound and inexhaustible subject that we cannot even begin to explore it in this book. We will simply review a few of the primary implications of this foundational truth and how it relates to our balance between temporal and eternal.

### Made in His Image

First of all, bearing the image of God means that men and women have a special *dignity* that the animals, and even the angels, do not. There are animals that are much bigger and stronger than human beings, but they are not made in God's image. The angels are marvelous supernatural creatures, intelligent and powerful, yet they too are never said to be created in His image. Wayne Grudem comments here:

> It will probably amaze us to realize that when the Creator of the universe wanted to create something "in his image," something more like himself than all the rest of the creation, he made us. This realization will give us a profound sense of dignity and significance...we are the culmination of God's infinitely wise and skillful works of creation. Even though sin has greatly marred that likeness, we nonetheless now reflect much of it and shall even more as we grow in likeness to Christ.[4]

Another result of being an image bearer is that mankind was given *dominion and authority* over the rest of the creation (Genesis 1:26-28; Psalm 8:6-8). Obviously, God has all authority, but in His sovereign wisdom, He has chosen to delegate a measure of it to humans. A third aspect of bearing His image is that men and women are *rational* beings and thus able to think and reason on a level that is distinct from and far superior to the animals. Fourth, human beings are also *moral* creatures who are accountable to their Creator-God and endowed with an innate sense of right and wrong.

Finally, and most compelling, the fact that men and women are made in God's image means that they are *spiritual* beings. Louis Berkhof makes this observation:

Another element usually included in the image of God is that of spirituality. God is Spirit, and it is but natural to expect that this element of spirituality also finds expression as the image of God...God "breathed into his nostrils the breath of life; and man became a living soul" (Genesis 2:7)...In view of this, we can speak of man as a spiritual being.[5]

*A Unique Relationship*
The fact that we are spiritual beings carries immense importance for our lives, both now and for eternity. This is the particular aspect of being an image-bearer that makes it possible for us to know God intimately, to communicate with Him, to worship Him, and to love Him in a way that is completely different from any other creature in the universe. Grudem again:

We have not only physical bodies but also immaterial spirits...This means that we have a spiritual life that enables us to relate to God as persons, to pray and praise him, and to hear him speaking his words to us...Connected with this spiritual life is the fact that we have immortality; we will not cease to exist but will live forever.[6]

It is evident, then, how being made in the image of our Creator relates to this temporal and eternal balance. God created us to be spiritual beings, and He also gave us a physical body in which we live and move. Thus, by God's design we are both spirit *and* body. For Christians, our physical bodies that die will eventually be resurrected and transformed, continuing to be a part of our existence with the Lord for eternity (1 Corinthians 15:44, 51-53; 1 Thessalonians 4:13-17).[7] Death then becomes nothing more than the supernatural gateway that ushers us from our temporal existence into our eternal one.

We therefore see here two unique things that physically exist in this world but are actually eternal: God's Word and people. In God's plan, they simultaneously belong to both the temporal and the eternal. The Word of God will live forever and so will the human beings who are created in His image.

Yet what about the rest of our lives? The overwhelming majority of what we say and do each day can generally be assigned to boxes that are clearly marked *temporal* or *eternal*. What are some of the factors we need to examine in order to find a healthy balance between these two vast areas of life?

## THE TEMPORAL BOX

Being mindful of and attentive to temporal things is imperative and serves several crucial purposes in our lives. First of all, it keeps us involved and ensures that we will fulfill the earthly responsibilities with which we have been entrusted: our family, our church, our work, our community. In Proverbs, we read this sage advice: "Know well the condition of your flocks, and give attention to your herds, for riches do not last forever" (27:23-24). While most of us in this day and time are not occupied with taking care of flocks and herds, we get the point. This verse is simply instructing us to work hard! For the believer, there is never a place for laziness or dishonesty. Whatever you do, give it your absolute best. Always strive for excellence. This principle applies not only to the workplace but to any position where you have been given responsibilities to fulfill. It could be a ministry at church, a volunteer position in a community organization, or any number of other opportunities. No matter what it is, no matter what task they are given, Christians should be known as people of integrity who do it well. In our dealings with others, we should always be diligent, wise, and gracious. Not only does this do the vital work of building character in our lives, but most of all it honors the One who has graciously granted us our abilities and talents.

### *Family Ties*

This principle of diligence applies to fulfilling our responsibilities within the family. We can learn many lessons from the woman described in Proverbs 31:10-31. She was one hard-working lady! She was eminently concerned with the well-being of her family, putting a great deal of time and effort into providing for them. Others outside the family were also recipients of her kindness and generosity. This woman is worth emulating since she is a prime example of someone who took her earthly responsibilities seriously and aimed for excellence in everything she did.

### *This Big, Beautiful World*

Being concerned about temporal things also serves another purpose. It reminds us to be aware of and grateful for God's glorious creation that we see all around us. While the Bible tells us in Revelation 21:1 that there will someday be a new heaven and a new earth, that does not diminish the fact that the current creation is *good*. As the biblical account of the Creation concludes in Genesis 1, we find this summary in verse 31: "And God saw everything that He had made, and behold, it was very good." The whole Creation is a reflection of the Lord's inherent goodness. Psalm 19:1 gives us this triumphant reminder: "The heavens declare the glory of God, and the sky above proclaims His handiwork." Every time I see a stunning sunrise or sunset, I am reminded that human artists can imitate this and create a beautiful picture on a canvas. Yet God is the Master Artist and the only One whose canvas is *the entire sky*, with His magnificent painting even changing moment to moment before our very eyes! What an awesome, incomprehensible God we have! Psalm 104 is another passage that is full of adoration for God's amazing Creation.

*Beware of Idolatry*

In this temporal world, our Father has generously given us beauty and art and music and a thousand other things to thrill our hearts. Still, we must guard against worshiping the *gifts* above the *Giver*; this is nothing less than idolatry. Too many times we revel in these things and totally divorce them from the Creator. We praise men and not God. Yet ultimately, it all comes from Him. *He* created beauty; *He* created music; *He* created art. They all originated in *His* incredibly infinite mind. Should not all these good gifts cause our hearts to burst forth in praise to the One who gave them in the first place? All that we see and experience in this world should always draw us back to our Creator.

## THE ETERNAL BOX

Clearly then, there is a time to think about temporal things. In addition, however, we also need to be thinking about heavenly things. There is a famous quote attributed to the nineteenth-century writer Oliver Wendell Holmes, Sr.: "Some people are so heavenly minded that they are no earthly good." Obviously, none of us wish to be described as "no earthly good." But here is the reality: we *must* be heavenly minded. We are given clear instruction in Colossians 3:2: "Set your minds on things that are above, not on things that are on earth." Because we have "eternity in our hearts" we must not neglect to pour ourselves into eternal things, which include our relationship with God and His Word and our relationships with other people.

*We Are Heavenly Expats*

The Word of God is replete with encouragement to focus our minds on heavenly things. Jesus told us in John 14 that He was going to prepare a place for us in His Father's house (14:2). Philippians 3:20 tells us that "our citizenship is in heaven, and from it we await a Savior, the Lord Jesus Christ." Just because we live here temporarily doesn't mean we *belong* here. Just because we have to be *in* the world doesn't mean we have to be *of* it. In 1 Peter, the apostle reassures us that we have "an inheritance that is imperishable, undefiled, and unfading, kept in heaven for you" (1:4). In 1 Timothy 6:7, we are given the wise reminder that "we brought nothing into this world and we cannot take anything out," which explains why Christ cautioned us to "not lay up for yourselves treasures on earth" (Matthew 6:19). We are repeatedly reminded in Scripture that the things of this earth are temporary and thus we must set our minds on the things that have eternal significance.

## THE GREAT FALLACY

Before we look at the possible ways we can be unbalanced in this area, I want to address a related issue here that is commonly called the "sacred and secular" divide. Basically, it is an attempt to subdivide the temporal world into two categories, with the sacred being more holy than the secular. The call to be a pastor or missionary would be considered higher or more spiritual than being called to be a doctor or accountant or truck driver; a church or seminary would be classified as a holy place while the workplace or a public park would be labeled as secular. Attending church or having personal devotions at home would be sacred activities; working at our job or attending a sports event would be thought of as secular.

Unfortunately, this is a false dichotomy that has crept into the collective thinking of the church. It is a completely wrong view of our life on this temporal earth. There are certainly clear contrasts between many things: obedience and disobedience, righteousness and unrighteousness, moral and immoral. But there is no such thing as sacred versus secular. Whatever the Lord's will is for our life, that is His calling for us. No matter what we do, we are to do it to the glory of God (1 Corinthians 10:31). Jesus exhorted us in Matthew 5:13-16 to be salt and light in a lost world. It is as important to share the gospel at your workplace as it is to proclaim it inside a church building! As believers who belong to Jesus Christ, we want to honor Him in every sphere of life. While we must be cautious about over-spiritualizing things, the reality is that our spiritual beliefs and perspectives as Christians *should* inform everything we do. The thought of God should never be far from our mind. When we truly understand this, we can worship and glorify God in every action or duty, no matter how routine or ordinary.

## PUTTING OUR EGGS IN THE WRONG BASKETS
### *The Empty Bag of Worldly Success*

Returning to our temporal/eternal balance, what a daunting task we then have of somehow charting a path between these two worlds! They both beckon to us, and we must somehow determine the proper balance for our lives. Let's begin by looking at the markers that can surface in our lives when we are too immersed in this earthly existence. First of all, we can put far too much emphasis on achievement and success and the amassing of fame and fortune (Hebrews 13:5; 1 John 2:15–16). We may find ourselves pursuing a type of self-fulfillment that chooses to disconnect itself from God and ignore the reality of His perfect, loving will for our lives. The emphasis shifts from pursuing God's glory to pursuing our own. It is an admirable thing to do our best and strive for excellence in our endeavors; it is another thing to get out of balance to the point that self-focused desires can literally begin to control our lives. Innumerable people have achieved their goals only to find that it was not enough; it did not bring the satisfaction they thought it would. Yet ironically, money and success and material possessions, these things that will someday pass away, are the very things that countless individuals look to for happiness and gratification in this life. If we are not careful, we can lose sight of the fact that true joy and fulfillment are found *only* in Christ (Psalm 107:9) and not in fleeting things such as worldly reputation or wealth. Jesus warned of this: "For what will it profit a man if he gains the whole world, and loses his own soul?" (Mark 8:36, NKJV) Our highest good and deepest contentment will always be found in knowing and worshipping our Lord and simply being who He has created us to be.

## Satisfaction Not Guaranteed

Following close behind the pursuit of wealth and success is an obsession with material things. The media constantly bombards us with the idea that we do not have *enough*. We set our minds on gaining possessions and begin to care far more than we should about our "stuff." Then, because we are overly focused on our possessions, it should not surprise us if we eventually become fearful and anxious about the possibility of losing them. The problem with this is that we fail to remember that it's all temporary. We forget that moth and rust destroy, and thieves can break through and steal (Matthew 6:19-20). No matter how valuable something is, it will not last forever. With the unrelenting passage of time, everything on this earth deteriorates. Given long enough, even the nicest clothes will become faded and worn out; shoes will get holes in them; cars will cease to run; houses will rot and collapse. Truly this is a "passing-away" world (1 Corinthians 7:31; 1 John 2:17).

## Save the Planet?

Another telltale sign of being too earthly minded is that we become excessively caught up in current environmental issues and causes, and the key word here is *excessive*. Should we guard what God has entrusted to us and take care of His beautiful creation? Certainly. Should we recycle whatever we can and avoid polluting our environment as much as possible? Why not? This is all simply part of our responsibility as conscientious citizens of the earth. Yet for some Christians, these temporal causes can become so all-consuming that it appears they've completely lost sight of the fact that Jesus will return to this earth someday, the former things will pass away, and there will be a new heaven and a new earth (2 Peter 3:10; Revelation 21:1). No matter how dedicated our conservation efforts might be, we are not going to change the course of history or override God's sovereign plan for the end times as revealed in His Word.

*Don't Be Fooled by Fads*

One last symptom of an excessive temporal focus is the tendency to become *overly* enamored of a particular philosophy or ideology. This is commonly seen in areas such as health, nutrition, and exercise where new ideas and discoveries seem to constantly be bursting on the scene. The areas of politics and schooling also seem to engender very strong loyalties to ideas and ways of thinking. And no one can deny that there is some good to be found in many of these endeavors and pursuits. For instance, in the area of health, is it profitable to engage in regular exercise? Of course. Countless scientific studies have proven the benefits of exercise. Is it worthwhile to put effort into eating foods that are healthy for our bodies and getting adequate sleep each night? Absolutely. All of this would fall under the heading of being a wise steward of the physical bodies

God has given us. Without question, there are a number of routines and habits that can be of temporary help to us. So it's perfectly acceptable to take advantage of these in order to live as healthy and productive a life as we possibly can, knowing this is a way to glorify our Creator. We must nevertheless acknowledge that no matter what we do or how beneficial our lifestyle may be, and no matter how it might appear otherwise from a human viewpoint, we will not ultimately alter the date of our death since it has already been set by the Lord! In Hebrews 9:27, we are told that "it is appointed unto men once to die" (KJV). We should endeavor to make prudent choices, all the while resting in the knowledge that God has predetermined the manner and time of our death and it will be accomplished exactly as He has planned. And there is great comfort to be found in that assurance.

Enthusiastic belief in a methodology that has proven to be personally helpful is of course understandable. It is concerning, however, when someone begins to give the impression that they believe some philosophy or practice is *the* answer or *the* right way to the exclusion of everything else. In addition, if the devotee's zeal is accompanied by an aggressive campaign to bring everyone else around to their viewpoint, this can definitely cause friction in inter-personal relationships. Remaining humble and discerning is crucial whenever we are introduced to new ideas and products and ways of doing things. Sometimes they're valid and worthwhile; sometimes they are nothing more than the latest fad. Time alone will tell. In John 14:6 we find the well-known scripture where our Lord declares, "I am the way, and the truth, and the life." Never forget that Jesus Christ *alone* can claim this; it would be heresy for any other person or philosophy or ideology to attempt to make that claim.

## HEAVENLY MYOPIA
### *Oblivious to Our Obligations*

As we look at the extremes on the other side, we recognize that it's also possible to be unbalanced in our preoccupation with the eternal. While being very attentive to spiritual things sounds good on the surface, if it's so excessively consuming that it causes us to minimize or ignore our God-given responsibilities, then this too can trigger all sorts of problems in our lives. An extreme example would be the man who insists on praying and studying his Bible all day long instead of working to provide for his family. Is it a good thing for him to pray and study God's Word? Of course. But not when that means his family lacks food or shelter or the necessities of life! We should always strive to find a wise and realistic balance that will enable us to fulfill our earthly obligations. Similarly, if we're so focused on eternal things that we neglect to pay a reasonable amount of attention to our material belongings, we can become unfaithful stewards of the possessions that the Lord has entrusted to us. Clothes need to be washed; houses need to be repaired and painted; grass needs to be mowed and yards should be kept neat; cars need to receive periodic maintenance to keep them running efficiently. When we ignore these mundane yet fundamental responsibilities of life, we are not only being negligent and inconsiderate of others but also showing a lack of gratitude for what we have been given by God.

## Don't Forget to Look at the Stars

Another symptom of being too heavenly minded is that we can become so preoccupied with the world that is yet to come that we completely miss the astounding beauty and majesty of *this* world. We must never forget to look around us and give our Creator the praise He is due for His incredible handiwork. Don't ever allow yourself to become jaded to the soaring grandeur of a lofty mountain or the breathtaking sight of countless stars in the night sky! Romans reminds us that God's "invisible attributes, namely, His eternal power and divine nature, have been clearly perceived, ever since the creation of the world, in the things that have been made" (1:20). The mighty God who paints the sky has actually revealed aspects of His character to us "in the things that have been made." We must not take this for granted.

## Sometimes We Weep

One final, and likely unintentional, manifestation of over-emphasizing the eternal would be the tendency to minimize the reality of suffering. Life in this fallen world can be painful and extremely difficult at times. Disappointment and heartaches and sickness and death are just a few of the vast array of trials that are part of the human condition. While we absolutely find comfort and hope in the eternal promises of God's Word, we must be careful not to use Bible verses indiscriminately like spiritual Band-Aids. In our well-intentioned efforts to comfort others, we can thoughtlessly fall back on spiritual clichés and platitudes that hurt more than they help. Never let your focus on the eternal be perceived as a lack of compassion for what the sufferer is experiencing. There is an appropriate time to remind a fellow believer of God's sovereignty and the eternal purposes being accomplished through their struggles. Yet there are other times when the most comforting thing we can do for someone is to say nothing at all and simply obey the command to "weep with those who weep" (Romans 12:15). Always seek to show compassion and bring comfort in the face of real suffering.

## LOOSENING OUR GRIP

We close our discussion with some parting instructions from the New Testament. An intriguing passage in 1 Corinthians gives valuable insight into how we should handle this challenging balance between the temporal and the eternal:

> But this I say, brethren, the time has been shortened, so that from now on those who have wives should be as though they had none; and those who weep, as though they did not weep; and those who rejoice, as though they did not rejoice; and those who buy, as though they did not possess; and those who use the world, as though they did not make full use of it; for the form of this world is passing away. (7:29-31, NASB)

The apostle Paul's point here is that even though we are compelled to interact and function in this earthly sphere, we must not live as if it were all there is. John Calvin, commenting on these verses, noted that Paul is urging us to use things in a disciplined way so that we are enabled to keep moving toward the goal.[8] Martin Luther had similar thoughts on this passage. Regarding how Christians should relate to the world, he states that they must "not sink too deeply into it either with love and desire or suffering and boredom, but should rather behave like guests on earth, using everything for a short time."[9] Luther here is emphasizing what is articulated in verse 31, that we should make use of this world but not *full* use of it. We must learn to hold the things of the world loosely, not allowing the griefs and joys, the trials and blessings of our earthly existence to define or overwhelm us.

In Paul's letter to Titus, we find more wise counsel on how we are to live in this physical world but still not lose sight of eternity. In the second chapter, he is clearly addressing temporal concerns when he exhorts us to "renounce ungodliness and worldly desires, and to live sensibly, righteously and godly in the present age" (2:12, NASB). But in verse 13 the apostle rightly balances this with the eternal by encouraging us to continue "looking for the blessed hope and the appearing of the glory of our great God and Savior, Christ Jesus" (2:13, NASB).

## THE EXTREMES

In summary, there are many notable signs that will help us determine if we are out of balance on either the temporal or eternal side. If you are overly focused on the *temporal*, here are some of the possible indicators:

- Overemphasis on worldly success and achievements
- Materialism—excessively preoccupied with possessions

- Fear/anxiety about potential losses
- Excessive preoccupation with temporal issues or causes
- Undue reliance on certain philosophies or ideologies (examples could be health, exercise, diet, politics, schooling methods, etc.)

On the other hand, if you're erring on the side of the *eternal*, you may see these symptoms:

- Neglect of God-given responsibilities
- Unfaithful stewardship of material possessions
- Lack of appreciation for the beauty of God's creation
- Lack of empathy and compassion for those who are suffering

As we saw earlier, what makes this such a complex balance is the fact that as human beings made in God's image, possessing both a spirit and a physical body, we truly have our feet in both worlds. The temporal calls loudly to us in the here and now and constantly demands our attention. Yet we hear the soft strains of the eternal wafting relentlessly through our souls, and we *know* there is something more waiting for us! In addition, when we belong to Christ, we are able to see with spiritual eyes and thus the eternal beckons us even more (2 Corinthians 5:1-7).

Perhaps no one has ever been more eloquent in describing our deep longing for the eternal than C. S. Lewis in *Mere Christianity*:

If I find in myself a desire which no experience in this world can satisfy, the most probable explanation is that I was made for another world. If none of my earthly pleasures satisfy it, that does not prove that the universe is a fraud. Probably earthly pleasures were never meant to satisfy it, but only to arouse it, to suggest the real thing. If that is so, I must take care, on the one hand, never to despise, or be unthankful for, these earthly blessings, and on the other, never to mistake them for the something else of which they are only a copy, or echo, or mirage. I must keep alive in myself the desire for my true country, which I shall not find till after death...I must make it the main object of life to press on to that other country and to help others to do the same.[10]

Mere Christianity, though not published until 1952, was based on a series of BBC radio talks from 1941 to 1944 when Lewis was a professor of English Literature at the University of Oxford. By the time the last of The Chronicles of Narnia was published in 1956, it would appear that this thought of "that other country" was still weighing heavy on his mind. In the final pages of The Last Battle, as the various characters leave the Shadowlands and make their way toward the new Narnia, the Unicorn cries ecstatically, "I have come home at last! This is my real country! I belong here. This is the land I have been looking for all my life, though I never knew it till now."[11] Of Peter and Edmund and Lucy, the main characters of the Narnia stories, the narrator says,

But for them it was only the beginning of the real story. All their life in this world and all their adventures in Narnia had only been the cover and the title page: now at last they were beginning Chapter One of the Great Story which no one on earth has read: which goes on forever: in which every chapter is better than the one before.[12]

Scripture clearly teaches that after death, those who love Christ will spend forever with Him in their *real* home, a home that waits patiently for each of us to complete our journey through this earthly existence (1 Corinthians 15:51-52; 1 Thessalonians 4:13-17; 1 Peter 1:4). As our days slip silently away from us and we find ourselves looking more and more toward the promise of eternity, how can our hearts not thrill to the exultant truth of Aslan's words at the close of *The Last Battle:* "The term is over: the holidays have begun."[13]

Keeping our balance between that which fades and that which lasts will require us to evaluate our earthly responsibilities carefully and make sure we are fulfilling them as we should. Spiritual endeavors and disciplines are also vital. We must remember what is eternal and let that drive us to God, to His Word, to prayer, and to ministry to others. As always, seeking godly input from other believers is invaluable as we make our way in this area.

# *For Personal Reflection and Application*

## CHAPTER 5—TEMPORAL AND ETERNAL

1.  What does Genesis 1:31 tell us about God's view of the physical world that He made? How should we view His creation? (Psalm 104:24; 145:3-5; 1 Timothy 4:4-5)

2.  What responsibility has God given to mankind in relation to the creation? (Genesis 2:15; Psalm 8:6) Which word, *ownership* or *stewardship*, best characterizes our relationship to all material things? What impact should this make on our attitude toward our possessions?

3.  What do Proverbs 27:23-27 and 31:13-27 tell us about some of the responsibilities we bear in this temporal world?

4.  What differences do you see in the values of those who lay up treasures on earth and those who lay up treasures in heaven? (Matthew 6:19-21) What is the relationship between our "treasure" and our hearts? How should remembering this keep us balanced as we make choices in life about where to invest our time and effort?

5.  Philippians 3:20 reminds us that if we know Christ, we are citizens of heaven. What are some of the characteristics of the inheritance

that awaits us there? (1 Peter 1:4) What "things above" should a believer focus on? (Colossians 3:1–4)

6. How does an eternal perspective protect us from being overanxious about our earthly possessions and the concerns of life in this world? (Matthew 6:25–34)

# ENDNOTES

1   Dictionary.com. (2019). "temporal." *Dictionary.com based on the Random House Unabridged Dictionary.* https://www.dictionary.com. Accessed October 5, 2019.

2   Ibid. "eternal."

3   Elliot, E. (2019). *Suffering is Never for Nothing* (Nashville, TN: B&H Publishing Group), 14.

4   Grudem, W. (1994). *Systematic Theology: An Introduction to Bible Doctrine* (Leicester, England: Inter-Varsity Press and Grand Rapids, MI: Zondervan Publishing House), 449.

5   Berkhof, L. (1939). *Systematic Theology* (Grand Rapids, MI: Wm. B. Eerdmans Publishing Co.), 204.

6   Grudem, *Systematic Theology: An Introduction to Bible Doctrine,* 446.

7   Ibid., 448.

8   Calvin, J. (2009). *Commentary on the Epistles of Paul the Apostle to the Corinthians* (Reprint, Grand Rapids, MI: Baker Books), 258.

9   Thiselton, A. C. (2000). *The First Epistle to the Corinthians: A Commentary on the Greek Text* (Grand Rapids, MI/Cambridge, U.K.: Wm. B. Erdman's Publishing), 584.

10  Lewis, C. S. (1952). *Mere Christianity* (New York: Macmillan), 120.

11  Lewis, C. S. (1956). *The Chronicles of Narnia* (New York: HarperCollins), 760.

12  Ibid., 767.

13  Ibid.

*Keep your heart with all vigilance, for
from it flow the springs of life.*
—Proverbs 4:23

*…that He would grant you…
to be strengthened with power
through His Spirit in the inner man…*
—Ephesians 3:16 (NASB)

*But I discipline my body and keep it under control…*
—1 Corinthians 9:27

*Rather train yourself for godliness; for
while bodily training is of some value,
godliness is of value in every way…*
—1 Timothy 4:7-8

*…women should adorn themselves
in respectable apparel,
with modesty and self-control…*
—1 Timothy 2:9

Chapter 6
# INNER MAN AND OUTER MAN

Car washing and auto detailing are worldwide, multi-billion-dollar industries, especially in countries where automobiles are a primary means of transportation. From custom car washes to high-end detail shops, the washing, cleaning, and polishing of vehicles is big business. In the United States alone, approximately 68,000 establishments brought in over $13 billion in revenue for 2019.[1] Likewise, the beauty and personal care industry is another massive enterprise estimated to be worth over $500 billion worldwide. This includes all skincare and personal care products, cosmetics, and fragrances. Again, in 2019, the sales just in the United States amounted to approximately $93.5 billion.[2] When you expand these estimates to incorporate the global revenue from all these industries, the figures are astronomical.

What do these entities have in common? They focus on the *outside* rather than the *inside*. Furthermore, the massive revenue they bring in reveals that people care a great deal about external appearance.

And yet the irony in all this is that, while we acknowledge that the concepts of *interior* and *exterior* both have their place, very few would deny that what is on the inside ultimately carries more weight. When it comes to an automobile, what is worse, a dented fender or a broken radiator? What will make the vehicle totally undrivable: a small area of chipped paint or a dead battery? Likewise, when it comes to our bodies, what is most significant: what we are like on the outside or what's happening on the inside? What will have the greatest effect on us: a bad haircut or a heart attack? What will actually matter most in the long term: that we've run out of our favorite perfume or that we were just diagnosed with a serious disease?

While the answers to these questions may be obvious, finding the balance in our lives between the internal and the external is not always as simple. In particular, the relationship between our *inner man* and *outer man* requires careful evaluation of the purpose and function of each. As we saw in chapter 5, when God created us in His image, He gave us an inner spirit that is invisible and a physical, material body that is not, and these are both worth a closer look.

Sometimes we find these two aspects of man juxtaposed in Scripture in a way that emphasizes the contrast between them. One familiar Old Testament verse comes from the story of the anointing of David by the prophet Samuel. Because of his disobedience, King Saul had been utterly rejected by God, and Samuel was thus commanded to go to Bethlehem to appoint the new king of Israel. As the narrative continues, we see the aged prophet initiating an encounter with David's father, Jesse, and David's seven older brothers. Impressed by the outward appearance of

David's oldest brother Eliab, Samuel exclaims, "Surely the Lord's anointed is before Him." His words prompted this important reminder from God that unlike us, our Creator evaluates people on a deeper level:

> But the LORD said to Samuel, "Do not look at his appearance or at the height of his stature, because I have rejected him; for God sees not as man sees, for man looks at the outward appearance, but the LORD looks at the heart." (1 Samuel 16:7)

In the New Testament, the apostle Paul also accentuates the difference between the internal and external aspects of man when he says he "joyfully concurs with the law of God in the inner man" but laments that he sees "a different law in the members of my body, waging war against the law of my mind" (Romans 7:22-23, NASB). Another notable illustration of this contrast is given by the apostle in 2 Corinthians 4. After acknowledging the reality of his own suffering earlier in the chapter and the inevitable decay of our outer physical bodies, Paul encourages his readers with the fact that no matter what the state of our body may be, our inner man can still be transformed daily by our faith and hope in the risen Christ:

> Therefore we do not lose heart, but though our outer man is decaying, yet our inner man is being renewed day by day. (4:16, NASB)

This is an intriguing verse. We all understand that in the natural world, the processes of decay and renewal stand diametrically opposed to one another. Yet in the Christian, they can actually coexist at the same time because of the reality that our inner and outer man, while connected in a mysterious and supernatural way, are still distinct from one another.

Since they therefore are not the same thing, both the inner man and the outer man are marked by a particular set of characteristics and also face their own particular set of temptations. Giving excessive attention to either one can create problems in our lives, and thus we see the necessity of striving for a biblical balance between the two. Let's begin our pursuit of this balance with a look at the faculties of the inner man.

## A LOOK AT THE INSIDE

Various terms are utilized in Scripture to describe the inner man. Depending on the emphasis of a specific verse, words such as *heart, mind, soul,* and *spirit* are all used interchangeably. As Craig Troxel points out, the word translated *heart* appears just under 1,000 times in the Bible and is used more than any other term to describe our inner self.[3] Yet this term is often misunderstood, as Troxel further explains:

> [T]he biblical understanding of the heart and our modern understanding of the heart are almost opposite. Today, heart is understood to refer to a person's emotions. Biblically, the heart refers to the whole person, including our capacity to think.[4]

The modern cultural tendency to relegate the heart to only the realm of emotions and how we "feel" reveals a woefully inadequate perception of what the Bible teaches in this area. A more complete comprehension is to see the inner man as consisting of various faculties such as our thoughts and perceptions, understanding and reasoning, intentions, imagination, conscience, desires and affections, emotions, and will.[5] All these various faculties relate to and work with each other continually. Every attitude and action, for good (Deuteronomy 6:5; 1 Kings 8:61; 1 Peter 1:22) or for evil (2 Chronicles 12:14; Jeremiah 17:9; Proverbs 6:18), is a result of the interplay between these various aspects of the inner man. When we truly begin to grasp all that is included here, it is not difficult to see its importance for our lives. This is why Paul prays that we will be "strengthened in our inner man" (Ephesians 3:16). This is also why Scripture is so indispensable to our lives, because as we are told in Hebrews 4:12, the living Word of God deals with "the thoughts and intentions of the heart."

So in contrast to the world's flawed understanding, the heart encompasses the sum total of who we are on the inside. Troxel summarizes it in this way:

> The scripture presents the heart not just as a unity but also as a trinity of spiritual functions: the mind, the desires, and the will. To put it another way, the heart includes what we "know" (our knowledge, thoughts, intentions, ideas, meditation, memory, imagination), what we "love" (what we want, seek, feel, yearn for), and what we "choose" (whether we will resist or submit, whether we will be weak or strong, whether we will say yes or no).[6]

Since everything we think, say, and do emanates from the heart, it is imperative that we guard it from the wrong influences. We are told in Scripture that "the Lord tests hearts" (Proverbs 17:3) and reminded that our hearts determine the very course of our lives: "Keep your heart with all diligence, for out of it spring the issues of life" (Proverbs 4:23). And because of these truths, we must acknowledge that the state of the inner man is crucial, not only for this life but for the life to come.

### *What About Our Emotions?*

Before we leave our discussion of the inner man, an additional word is needed here regarding our emotions or how we "feel." Since all the faculties of the inner man work together, it is best to think of our emotions as being the result of their combined influence. In other words, it is our thinking, affections, and so on that govern our emotions. Therefore, cultivating biblical thinking and desires and choosing to live by faith in God will produce appropriate and controlled emotions.

It is true, of course, that based upon our natural "wiring" and also based upon assorted life experiences, some people have a personality that is more stoic, and some people tend to be more emotional. We should appreciate the Lord's wisdom and creativity as seen in the variety of people around us. Moreover, this should be a helpful reminder that while we all have thoughts and emotions, they may be manifested differently in various individuals. The sovereignty of God is at play here in the unique personality we each have developed, along with our own intrinsic set of strengths and weaknesses.

Regardless of our personality, however, we should always strive to be sympathetic, empathetic people. Whether we are naturally more analytical and reserved or on the other hand more emotionally expressive, we should all weep with those who weep and rejoice with those who rejoice (Romans 12:15). James Montgomery Boice comments on the caring heart of our Savior during His earthly ministry: "Jesus wept and thus revealed a God who enters into the anguish of His people and grieves with them in their afflictions."[7] The Lord obviously expressed emotions. It is right to conclude, then, that emotions are a part of what it means for us to be made in the image of God.

The reality we must be aware of, though, is the undeniable fact that our emotions can fluctuate. We therefore cannot trust feelings as an infallible guide to making decisions in life. In fact, those who live by their emotions may be more susceptible to *mysticism,* which is an approach to the Christian life that is based upon subjective feelings, impressions, and experiences. The danger in mysticism is that there are no objective standards, with the result being that we can essentially reach whatever conclusions we want. The Word of God, which never changes, is thus critical as the mooring that keeps us tethered to truth and enables us to exercise wisdom and discernment (Psalm 19:7-9; John 17:17). It is biblical truth that produces right thinking and affections, and these in turn will produce God-honoring emotions.

## A LOOK AT THE OUTSIDE

While the inner man is undoubtedly of prime importance because it determines the "issues of life," we nevertheless cannot underestimate the significance of our outer man. Understanding the external is in some ways an easier endeavor. In its most basic definition, it is simply our physical, material body which has been given to us by God. It is what we and others see on the outside, as compared to the spiritual inner man, which is invisible.

We must, however, be careful to not reduce the inner man to just being "housed" in a certain part of our physical body; this is an inaccurate view of the relationship between these two aspects of man. The inner man and outer man are distinct from one another but not separate. We exist as holistic beings, therefore the inner and outer man are inextricably intertwined in our person. Thus we are more than just the sum of our parts. Wayne Grudem comments:

> It is important to recognize that it is *man himself* who is created in the image of God, not just his spirit or mind. Certainly our physical bodies are a very important part of our existence and, as transformed when Christ returns, they will continue to be a part of our existence for all eternity.[8]

At the moment of our death, for the very first time since we were created in our mother's womb, our spirit and our body will actually be separated from each other. But Scripture teaches us that even this separation will be temporary, and someday our spirit will be reunited with our resurrected, spiritual body (1 Corinthians 15:42-44, 51-53; Philippians 3:20-21).

*Our Hearts Revealed*

One of the fundamental reasons the outer man is so significant is because it is the visible vehicle through which the faculties of the inner man are all expressed. We cannot, therefore, minimize its importance, as Grudem further explains:

> Our bodies therefore have been created by God as suitable instruments to represent in a physical way our human nature, which has been made to be like God's nature. In fact, almost everything we do is by means of the use of our physical bodies— our thinking, our moral judgments, our prayer and praise, our demonstrations of love and concern for each other—all are done using the physical bodies God has given us.[9]

The profound principle that the inner man is expressed through the outward man is clearly taught by Jesus. In Matthew 12, He seized upon the analogy of a tree and the type of fruit it produces to perfectly illustrate His point about the visible manifestation of what resides in the human heart:

> Either make the tree good and its fruit good, or make the tree bad and its fruit bad, for the tree is known by its fruit...How can you speak good, when you are evil? For out of the abundance of the heart the mouth speaks. The good person out of his good treasure brings forth good, and the evil person

out of his evil treasure brings forth evil. (Matthew 12:33-35)

In Mark 7, Christ again spoke sobering words about the heart of man and the sinful attitudes and actions that can proceed from it:

And he said, "What comes out of a person is what defiles him. For from within, out of the heart of man, come evil thoughts, sexual immorality, theft, murder, adultery, coveting, wickedness, deceit, sensuality, envy, slander, pride, foolishness. All these evil things come from within, and they defile a person." (Mark 7:18-23)

Thankfully, in contrast, the heart that *loves* God will also be clearly manifested in external ways. A heart that is fixed on God will long for Him and seek His face (Psalm 27:8; 42:1-2; 63:1; 84:2; 119:10); will sing and give praise (Psalm 57:7); will proclaim Him to others (Psalm 9:1); will keep His Word and bear fruit (Luke 8:15); will do His will (Psalm 40:8; Ephesians 6:6); will endeavor to avoid sin (Psalm 119:11); will walk in His statutes and keep his commandments (1 Kings 8:61; Psalm 119:10,34); will love other Christians and minister to them (Ephesians 4:32; 1 Peter 1:22); and will reflect the love of God and the patience of Christ (2 Thessalonians 3:5, NKJV).

The bottom line is this: our lives on the outside will inevitably reflect who we really are on the inside, for good or for bad. To say it differently, our hearts will reveal themselves over time; the truth of who we are, what we believe, and who or what we worship will be made abundantly clear to those around us. As believers, we are to live holy lives (1 Peter 1:14-16). We are to walk wisely in this world, as "children of light" (Ephesians 5:8-10, 15-16; 1 Thessalonians 5:5; Philippians 2:15). Our external bodies therefore play a vital role in what kind of testimony we present, not only to fellow believers but also to those who do not know Christ.

### Reflecting Our Creator

Our outer man fulfills other purposes as well. Besides enabling us to minister and do good to others, our bodies also provide us with another means through which to express the fact that we are created in God's image. What an amazing thought—not only do our hearts echo the image of God but our bodies do as well! Grudem is again helpful with his thought-provoking observation that although God is spirit and therefore does not possess a body, yet He created our bodies in such a way that they would actually reflect something of His own character:

> For example, our physical bodies give us the ability to see with our eyes. This is a Godlike quality because God himself sees, and sees far more than we will ever see, although he does not do it with physical eyes like we have. Our ears give us the ability to hear and this is a Godlike ability, even though God does not have physical ears...our mouths give us the ability to speak, reflecting the fact that God is a God who speaks. Our senses of taste and touch and smell give us the ability to understand and enjoy God's creation, reflecting the fact that God himself

understands and enjoys his creation, though in a far greater sense than we do.[10]

*The Responsibility of Stewardship*

One final nuance of why our bodies have significance falls under the heading of stewardship. Being mindful of our health and taking care of the body God has entrusted to us is a fitting way to honor Him and convey our gratitude. While we recognize that the Lord has sovereignly determined the span of our lives, we cannot know how many years He has planned for us. It is a worthy endeavor, therefore, to put reasonable effort into keeping our bodies strong and active for the purpose of serving Him and other people.

## TOO SELF-FOCUSED TO BE HAPPY

Now that we have briefly examined the legitimate purposes and functions of the inner and outer man, what are the dangers that come from going to the extreme on either side? If an individual tends to focus excessively on the inner man, a predictable danger is a growing self-absorption that becomes unhealthy and crowds out the ability to care for others. No one enjoys being around people who think only of themselves! The far end of this spectrum, what some would label "narcissism," is characterized by an arrogant sense of self-importance, a need for excessive admiration, and a lack of empathy for other people. While most individuals fall far short of this extreme, they can still fall into the trap of being overly occupied with their own thoughts and opinions, their feelings, their dreams and goals, their hurts and disappointments. Everything is about them! They can become so introspective they literally have no time or inclination to think about others.

The amazing paradox for a person like this is that the more he seeks happiness by focusing on self, generally the more unhappy he becomes. Why is this so? Because of our ongoing struggle with sin, the tendency of the human heart is to dwell on what we *don't* have rather than what we *do*. This traces all the way back to the Garden of Eden, when Satan directed Eve's attention to what she didn't have rather than what she did, and that dynamic has never changed. The more we think about what we want but don't have, the more unhappy we become. It begins to take us down a dead-end street of self-pity that can end in depression and despair. The most self-focused people are usually the most miserable.

Similarly, there is an ironic paradox to be found in people who complain that all their problems are rooted in the fact that they have low self-worth or low self-esteem. The reality, however, is the exact opposite: they actually have very high self-esteem, which is made evident by the amount of time and effort they invest into focusing on themselves! David Wells writes that our cultural emphasis on self-esteem began to be more pronounced in America in the 1960s and a new worldview emerged during this time. He makes the case that people began to turn more and more inward, and for many it became the norm that life was all about esteeming yourself and discovering your inner potential for your own benefit. Wells states: "It is not unreasonable to think that this turn in our culture would have found resistance among the religious...but evangelicals fell headlong into this new way of seeing life."

And sadly, many decades later, the language of self-esteem and every other kind of self-love has become a dominant theme in our culture.[11]

In contrast to all this insecurity and self-focus, the person whose heart belongs to God has the Spirit-given ability to be completely content and secure in his inner man. We acknowledge that we are sinners, yet we are assured that we have been given *infinite* worth simply because we are made in God's image and because He has made each of us unique. Moreover, placing our faith in Christ's atoning work on the cross enables us to know God's amazing love and forgiveness in this world and to have eternal security in the next (Ephesians 1:7-8; 2:6-7). Ian Hamilton comments:

> It is a constant ploy of the devil to absorb us with ourselves; to turn the Christian faith into an exercise in the acquiring of self-esteem. Our great weapon against his insidious, self-promoting, Christ-dishonouring tactics, is to live out the connection between God's justification of the ungodly through faith alone in Jesus Christ, and the relationship every believer now enjoys with God on account of that: "Therefore, since we have been justified by faith, we have peace with God through our Lord Jesus Christ."[12]

### The Middle Ground

Again, we must not forget there is a healthy balance to be found here. It is not wrong to pursue our goals and dreams and seek to make a difference while we are here on this earth. It is not wrong to use our gifts and abilities and strive for excellence in all we do. There is a reasonable degree of attention that *must* be given to the inner man since it is imperative that we make decisions and function in daily life—yet a biblical perspective still needs to be maintained.

### The Key to Joy

This sinful, broken world will never bring us true peace or happiness; we therefore should not waste time focusing on ourselves and what we supposedly lack. Instead, we can choose to turn our attention toward our Creator and the people around us, and the wonderful side effect of this choice is a blessed self-forgetfulness. I can personally affirm that the happiest people I know are the ones who waste very little time thinking about themselves. They are too busy setting their minds on higher and nobler things (Colossians 3:2). Instead of pleasing self, their supreme goal is to please God and glorify Him (2 Corinthians 5:9; Psalm 115:1). Spending our lives loving and serving the Lord and other people paves a sure path to joy (Psalm 16:11; 119:11; Isaiah 58:10-11). Martyn Lloyd-Jones, in his book *Spiritual Depression*, explains the difference between happiness and joy: we cannot make ourselves happy, but we can always rejoice in the Lord, no matter our circumstances. Then he concludes with this wise counsel:

> Set your whole aim upon righteousness and holiness and as certainly as you do so you will be blessed, you will be filled, you will get the happiness you long for. Seek for happiness and you will never find

it, seek righteousness and you will discover you are happy…it will be there…without your seeking it.[13]

John Piper reminds us that Jesus said it is more blessed to give than to receive (Acts 20:35) and urges us to remember that "God has made us to flourish by being spent for others."[14] Milton Vincent contributes to our discussion with his thoughts on the difference the gospel makes in our lives and how it rescues us from being excessively focused on self. Marveling at God's love for His children, Vincent observes, "Thankfully, the gospel frees me from the shackles of self-love…His astonishing love for me renders self-absorption moot and frees me up to move on to causes and interests far greater than myself."[15]

### Paralyzed in Ministry

Another danger we can fall into is that of being too introspective and too analytical when it relates to serving others. I have known a handful of individuals who had cultivated a habit of "overthinking" their motives in ministry. They were excessively concerned about *why* they were doing what they were doing. These were the questions they wrestled with: *Is my purpose in doing this to draw attention to myself? Am I secretly trying to impress someone? Am I doing it out of guilt? Am I trying to build up my self-esteem?* Because they spent an inordinate amount of time obsessing over these issues, constantly afraid they were ministering for the wrong reasons, the end result was that they never did much of anything for others. They essentially became paralyzed by their own inward focus. If you struggle with this tendency, pray that the Holy Spirit will work in your heart to help you forget about yourself and enable you to turn your attention toward other people.

### Don't Ignore The Outside

One final effect of being too inwardly focused is the possibility of giving too little attention to the outer man. Undoubtedly, the greater problem in our society is that we tend to put too *much* emphasis on externals, but we can also be extreme in the other direction. Melody Green commented on this many years ago in her short booklet on modesty:

> I have seen people go to the other extreme and try to prove to others that they are more spiritual because of their *lack* of concern about the way they look. But this too can be just another form of pride and self-righteousness.[16]

A complete lack of concern about your external appearance is not a sign of spirituality. It can actually be distracting and a poor testimony. We should therefore put a reasonable amount of effort toward being presentable to those around us. The balance is that we should not pay too much attention to our outer man, but on the other hand we shouldn't pay too little either!

## THE DANGEROUS DELUSION

This now leads us to examine the extremes on the other side, which is being too preoccupied with our outer man. As we saw in the introduction to this chapter, our world is obsessed with externals. To many, appearance and image and persona are the things that matter most and whether there is actually something behind them is of secondary importance. In a culture of shallowness, the mere illusion of substance is enough to satisfy a great many people. There is an old expression about "having more in the show window than in the warehouse," and regrettably, the "show window" mentality is alive and well in our society today. Vanity and superficiality are commonplace and accepted as normal. Unfortunately, social media has contributed greatly to this problem, with the ability to project an image that may have very little basis in reality.

We see this focus on externals everywhere we turn. When dealing with outward appearance, cosmetics and photoshopping a picture can go a long way in making someone look significantly better than they do in reality. When related to character, the sad reality is that if you can make yourself look good, you don't really have to *be* good. As long as you give the impression of honesty, you don't actually have to *be* honest. No matter what earthly category we might consider—business, politics, religion, entertainment, advertising—the seductive power of *image* cannot be overstated. As believers, though, we must realize that the Bible teaches us the exact opposite. Scripture makes it very clear that our inner man is of first importance; character and integrity are absolutely essential (Psalm 15:1-5; Micah 6:8; Titus 3:1-2). It also reminds us that physical beauty will fade (Proverbs 31:30) and moth and rust will corrupt (Matthew 6:19-21). We must, therefore, continually resist being caught up in this worldly mindset that places so much emphasis on what we see on the outside.

One of the main things we need to guard against here is obsessing too much about our external appearance and thus spending a disproportionate amount of time (or money) on our outer man. This is an indicator that our priorities have strayed from the biblical pattern of the significance of the inner man. Without question, we should be mindful of our physical health and strive to be good stewards of our bodies as best we can. Common sense tells us to make wise decisions in the basic areas of nutrition, exercise, and rest, and avoid any life habits that can harm us. In his first epistle to Timothy, Paul acknowledges that "bodily exercise profits a little" (1 Timothy 4:8, NKJV). In 3 John 2, the apostle John prayed for Gaius that he would "prosper and be in good health." Physical wholeness and well-being is a legitimate, reasonable goal. Yet this goal can so quickly devolve into an idol of the heart and become a prideful desire to draw attention to self or impress others with our fitness or our physique. Examining our motives honestly in this area therefore is imperative.

## Modesty Matters

A significant area related to external appearance, especially for Christian women (though this applies to men as well), is the matter of modesty. It is no secret that we live in an incredibly immodest world. In her insightful book *The Look*, Nancy DeMoss Wolgemuth summarizes some of the stark differences between the world's perspective on this subject and the instruction we find in God's Word. The world says that beauty is external and physical; the Bible teaches us that beauty is internal and spiritual. The world insists that we should dress for people to notice us;

God tells us that we are to dress in a way that glorifies Him. Lastly, the world would say the purpose of clothing is to uncover and reveal; yet from the time that God created clothing for Adam and Eve in the Garden, it is clear that the purpose is to cover and conceal.[17]

It is overwhelmingly apparent that our popular culture is strongly opposed to the biblical standard, and this places tremendous pressure on women to yield to the immodesty of the day. Yet Romans 12:1 tells us that we are not to be conformed to this world, and this includes the way we dress. We have been given clear instruction from the Bible in this area. In 1 Timothy 2:9, women are instructed to "adorn themselves with proper clothing, modestly and discreetly." In the apostle Peter's first epistle, he gives this exhortation: "Your adornment must not be merely external...but let it be the hidden person of the heart, with the imperishable quality of a gentle and quiet spirit, which is precious in the sight of God" (1 Peter 3:3-4, NASB). These verses not only entreat us to dress appropriately but also to cultivate an inner beauty that is infinitely more valuable in God's sight.

If we are to think biblically on this topic, a foundational principle to remember is that if we know Christ, we have been bought with a price and our body is the temple of the Holy Spirit (1 Corinthians 6:20; 7:23). And because these things are true, it follows that we should dress in a way that honors Him. It helps to think about it this way: we are dressing a body that actually belongs to God; it doesn't belong to us anymore! So ultimately, how we dress is all about the glory of God, just as everything in our lives should be.

In a number of ways, this goal of glorifying God protects both us and the other people in our lives. First of all, the desire to please Him will motivate us to regularly examine our hearts for sinful motives in this area. Second, it will keep us from using our appearance for all the wrong reasons: to pridefully attract attention to ourselves, to gain acceptance or approval, or to attempt to somehow manipulate others through the way we dress. Third, it will be a blessing to others if we put mindful effort into not being a distraction or a source of visual temptation.

## A Further Word to Women

One of the main reasons that modesty is necessary, especially for women, is because of the way in which we are tempted. Surely we have noticed that men and women are different! And while there are always exceptions, in general men tend to be more visual and more affected by what they *see*. This is one of the main reasons the pornography industry has historically been aimed at men. Pastor Kent Keller explains that men "are more drawn by what they see in real life or pictures, while women are more drawn by emotional relationships."[18] Wolgemuth passes along the significant insight that "what a man's touch is to a woman, the sight of a woman is to a man."[19] King David was tempted when he saw Bathsheba bathing (2 Samuel 11:2). Job said he made a covenant to guard his eyes and not look upon a young woman (Job 31:1). Sight, therefore, is a powerful channel through which men can be enticed to sinful imaginations and sexual sin. As believing women, we therefore have a responsibility to not intentionally dress in a manner that will be a stumbling block to our Christian brothers (1 Corinthians 8:9). In this modern world, men are tempted by sensuality everywhere they look—television, movies, billboards, magazines, the internet—and the never-ending barrage of suggestive images drives them into a constant battle to keep their minds pure. Should Christian men not be able to rest for just a short time when they are around the women at church? Should they not be provided a brief respite from the relentless temptation they deal with every day?

Let me be very clear here that immodesty is not an excuse for lust. A man cannot control what women wear, but he *can* control what he looks at. Ultimately, it is the man's responsibility to guard his eyes and heart from temptation. But as their sisters in Christ, we should do our best to help them. Wolgemuth makes a great statement here:

> This isn't to suggest that men aren't responsible for their thought life or their behavior. They are. And they have to learn how to walk with God and bring those thoughts under the control of Christ even though they live in a culture where immodesty is rampant. However, as Christian women, our clothing choices can either *help* men succeed morally or can put temptation in their path that they may find it difficult to overcome. That means both men <u>and</u> women are responsible for moral purity!... We should do everything in our power to help our brothers stand and to be sure that our dress and appearance bring glory to God.[20]

*Check Your Heart*

One of the most helpful tools I've ever found on this subject is the "Modesty Heart Check," written by Carolyn Mahaney and her daughter Nicole Mahaney Whitacre. It is a very practical checklist to help women accurately assess the clothes they wear each day (and the principles are also applicable to jewelry, cosmetics, and so on.) I especially appreciate the focus on the heart in the opening paragraphs and the insightful questions they encourage us to ask ourselves: *What statement do my clothes make about my heart? In choosing what clothes to wear today, whose attention do I desire and whose approval do I crave? Am I seeking to please God or impress others? Is what I wear consistent with biblical values of modesty, self-control and respectable apparel, or does my dress reveal an inordinate identification and fascination with sinful cultural values?*[21]

As we have already discussed in this chapter, the outer man is actually just a reflection of our inner man; therefore, the key question is not "What do I wear?" but "What is the state of my heart?" How we present ourselves on the *outside* reveals a great deal about who we are on the *inside*. When we enter a room, before we ever say a word, our clothes (and anything else external) are already making a statement. In Matthew 12:34, Jesus said that "out of the abundance of the heart the mouth speaks." We could also apply this overall principle to the issue of modesty and say, "Out of the abundance of the heart *the body dresses*." A godly woman many years ago passed on this exhortation to the young women in her church: "Our character is the picture, our appearance is the frame; our frame should complement the picture, not distract from it."[22] These are wise words for us to ponder.

In summary, here are three important truths to keep in mind. Our bodies belong to God (1 Corinthians 6:20; 7:23; 2 Corinthians 6:16); our outward appearance reflects our inner condition (Matthew 12:34-35; Proverbs 6:14); and we have a responsibility to not be a stumbling block to others (1 Corinthians 8:9). We should put reasonable effort into our appearance so we are not a distraction, and we should also be careful to not adorn ourselves in a way that is immodest or designed to attract attention. Our goal should always be God's glory and not our own.

### *The Appeal to the Flesh*

Another risk of an external focus is that we can become *overly* enamored of the pleasures that we can experience in this world with our physical bodies. These pleasures can include food, drink, entertainment, and a host of other activities. In his second epistle to Timothy, Paul refers to those who are "lovers of pleasure rather than lovers of God" (2 Timothy 3:2). And though this statement primarily characterizes unregenerate people, the love of pleasure can even be a subtle temptation for the Christian. While we are certainly free to enjoy many of the blessings of this temporal world (see chapter 3), the balance is that we must discipline our bodies in a way that honors the Lord and also be wise in how we manage our time (1 Corinthians 9:27). Even good things that are allowed can become idols in our hearts if we love them too much. Paul explained that while all things were lawful for him, not everything was edifying and therefore he would not "be mastered by anything" (1 Corinthians 6:12; 10:23, NASB). Even if something is not sinful, it is still vital that we keep first things first and not allow it to distract us from what is truly valuable in life. We must never allow a desire for physical pleasure and enjoyment to overshadow or diminish our love for God and eternal things.

### Don't Be A Pharisee

One last danger of an excessive emphasis on externals is that it breeds hypocrisy, which is a deadly disconnect between the inner and outer man. During His earthly ministry, Jesus strongly and repeatedly condemned the Pharisees for their arrogance and self-righteousness. Matthew 23 paints a devastating picture of these religious leaders. They cared a great deal about outward appearances and the praise of men (vv. 5-7). Claiming to love God's law, they put heavy burdens on others but refused to obey it themselves (vv. 3-4). They majored on minors and ignored the weightier matters of the law (vv.23-24). Their hypocrisy was clearly exposed by Jesus' words: "Woe to you, scribes and Pharisees, hypocrites! For you clean the outside of the cup and the plate, but inside they are full of greed and self-indulgence...First clean the inside of the cup and the plate, that the outside also may be clean...For you are like whitewashed tombs, which outwardly appear beautiful, but within are full of dead people's bones and all uncleanness. So you also outwardly appear righteous to others, but within you are full of hypocrisy and law-lessness" (vv. 25-28).

This type of duplicity is embodied in pretending to believe what we don't, and in verbally giving the impression we adhere to a certain principle when our behavior does not support it. The word *hypocrite* aptly derives from the Greek word "hypokrites" which means "pretender" or "actor"—a perfect description. Not only can we be guilty of this ourselves, those of us who are parents must be very careful not to encourage this in our children. When we only deal with external behavior and refuse to tackle underlying heart issues, we are unintentionally encouraging the attitude of Pharisaism in our children, and this can be disastrous. This could even lay the early groundwork for a life characterized by a lack of honesty and integrity. Parents, don't be pacified by external conformity that cloaks a rebellious spirit. Always deal with the deeper concerns such as pride, selfishness, anger, dishonesty, and ingratitude. Our children can be so well-behaved and look so good on the outside—and yet be so lost on the inside.

## THE EXTREMES

We must remain vigilant and alert to the symptoms that can appear in our lives when we drift into an excessive focus on either the inner or outer man. If you are excessive in your emphasis on the *inner man*, these are the possible signs:

- Morbid introspection/self-focus/self-absorption
- Paralysis (excessive concern about motives)
- Sloppiness or slovenliness

Being too preoccupied with the *outer man* can lead to these problems in your life:

- Wrong priorities
- Vanity/shallowness/externalism
- Immodesty
- Excessive desire for physical experiences or pleasure
- Pharisaism/hypocrisy

In Romans 12, we are given this exhortation by the apostle Paul:

> I appeal to you therefore, brothers, by the mercies of God, to present your bodies as a living sacrifice, holy and acceptable to God, which is your spiritual worship. Do not be conformed to this world, but be transformed by the renewal of your mind, that by testing you may discern what is the will of God, what is good and acceptable and perfect. (12:1-2)

Being transformed in our inner man and presenting our body as a living sacrifice presents a balanced picture of what our goal should be in this area. As always, it is essential that we seek the help of the Holy Spirit in prayer and Bible study as we endeavor to faithfully live out these truths in our lives.

## *For Personal Reflection and Application*

### CHAPTER 6—INNER MAN AND OUTER MAN

1. In 1 Samuel 16:7 and 2 Corinthians 4:16 we see the two aspects of man. What are some of the other words used in Scripture to refer to the inner man? (Psalm 51:10; 19:14; Isaiah 26:9; Matthew 22:37; Galatians 6:18; Ephesians 4:23)

2. Proverbs 4:23 exhorts us to "guard our hearts." Why is this so crucial and what are some of the practical ways we can do this?

3. What are the consequences of being too focused on the inner man? Prayerfully examine your heart to determine if there are areas where you struggle with being too self-focused. Identify some steps you can take to be more balanced.

4. Christian women are given clear instruction about their outer appearance in 1 Timothy 2:9–10 and 1 Peter 3:4. In your own words, explain why modesty matters and how immodest dress can be a distraction or a temptation to those around us.

5. From 1 Peter 3:4, what inner quality of a godly woman is precious to God? Describe what this means in your own words.

6. What are the chief dangers of being too outwardly focused? Are there areas in your life
   where your find yourself too concerned with
   external appearances? How can you stay balanced in those areas?

# ENDNOTES

1   IBISWorld. (2020). "Car Wash & Auto Detailing in the US industry outlook (2020-2025)." https://www.ibisworld.com/united-states/market-research-reports/car-wash-auto-detailing-industry/. Accessed May 30, 2020.

2   Cvetlovska, L. (2019). "45 Beauty Industry Statistics That Will Impress You." *LoudCloud Health* (January 8). https://loudcloud-health.com/beauty-industry-statistics/. Accessed May 30, 2020.

3   Troxel, A. C. (2020). *With All Your Heart* (Wheaton, IL: Cross-way,), 17.

4   Ibid., 18.

5   Vine, W. E., Unger, M. F., and White, W. Jr. (1985). *Vine's Expository Dictionary of Biblical Words* (Nashville, TN: Thomas Nelson, Inc.), 297.

6   Troxel. *With All Your Heart,* 20.

7   Boice, J. M. (1999). *The Gospel of John,* 5 vols. (Grand Rapids: Baker), 3:874.

8   Grudem, W. (1994). *Systematic Theology: An Introduction to Bible Doctrine* (Leicester, England: Inter-Varsity Press and Grand Rapids, MI: Zondervan Publishing House), 448.

9   Ibid.

10  Grudem. *Systematic Theology,* 448.

11  Wells, D. (2008). *The Courage to be Protestant* (Grand Rapids, MI: Wm. B. Erdmans Publishing Co.), 136–38.

12  Hamilton, I. (2013). *The Faith-Shaped Life* (Carlisle, PA: The Banner of Truth Trust), 37–38.

13  Lloyd-Jones, M. (1965). *Spiritual Depression: Its Causes and Its Cures* (Grand Rapids, MI: Wm. B. Erdmans Publishing Co), 115–17.

14  Piper, J. (2006). *When the Darkness Will Not Lift* (Wheaton, IL: Crossway Books), 63.

15  Vincent, M. (2008). *A Gospel Primer for Christians* (Bemidji, MN: Focus Publishing), 30.

16  Green, M. (1980). *Uncovering the Truth about Modesty* (Lindale, TX: Last Days Ministries).

17  Wolgemuth, N. D. (2003). *The Look: Does God Really Care What I Wear* (Buchanan, MI: Revive Our Hearts), 17.

18  Martha Peace and Kent Keller, *Modesty: More Than a Change of Clothes* (Phillipsburg, NJ: P&R Publishing, 2015), 24.

19  Wolgemuth. *The Look,* 24.

20  Ibid., 20–21.

21  Mahaney, C., and Mahaney Whitacre, N. (2005). *Girl Talk: Mother-Daughter Conversations on Biblical Womanhood* (Wheaton, IL: Crossway Books), 205.

22  Keasling, S. (1991). Grace Community Church, Sun Valley, CA.

*For man is born for trouble, as sparks fly upward.*
—Job 5:7 (NASB)

*"In the world you will have tribulation."*
—John 16:33

*But understand this, that in the last days
there will come times of difficulty.*
—2 Timothy 3:1

*…knowing that the same kinds of
suffering are being experienced by your
brotherhood throughout the world.*
1 Peter 5:9

*And we know that for those who love God
all things work together for good…*
—Romans 8:28

*May the God of hope fill you with all joy and
peace in believing, so that by the power of
the Holy Spirit you may abound in hope.*
—Romans 15:13

*…Christ Jesus, [who is] our hope…*
—1 Timothy 1:1 (NASB)

## Chapter 7
# REALITY AND HOPE

Military history is replete with accounts of disastrous battles where overconfidence and underestimation of the enemy were significant factors. In these instances, reality becomes a casualty of undue optimism and unreasonable hope. One of these was a famous six-week battle in World War II called the Battle of the Bulge. This took place in the Ardennes Forest in Belgium in the bitter winter of 1944–45, only months before the end of the war. This last major German offensive of the war in Europe was an attempt to split the Allied lines as they advanced toward Germany, with the goal of forcing a peace treaty in favor of Germany and its allies. As the attack progressed, the Allied line took on the appearance of a large "bulge," thus giving the conflict its name.[1] The German attack came as a total surprise due to a combination of Allied overconfidence, preoccupation with their own offensive plans, and overcast weather conditions that grounded their air forces. Complicating matters for the Allies were severe supply problems and exhausted troops. Finally, the German attack was strategically directed at a weakly defended section of the Allied front. While the offensive was ultimately unsuccessful and the Allied forces claimed victory on January 25, 1945, it was a brutal and costly battle for both sides.[2]

Another lesser-known military event in history took place one hundred years before World War II and is commonly labeled the 1842 retreat from Kabul, also known as the "Massacre of Elphinstone's Army." This was another tragic incident where reality fell prey to foolish decisions. The British army had occupied the city of Kabul in 1839 during the first Anglo-Afghan War; however, in January 1842, a deteriorating situation eventually forced the acting commander, Major General William Elphinstone, to withdraw his forces to another British garrison 90 miles away. The assumption was that they would be able to escape Kabul without incident, but reality proved otherwise. As the column of 4,500 army troops and 12,000 associated civilians attempted to retreat, they were continually attacked and ambushed by the Afghan forces; the massive company was virtually annihilated in the span of just one week. One of the few survivors, Lt. Vincent Eyre, noted that senior military leaders had largely ignored warnings of the security situation on the ground and the military's unpreparedness in Kabul.[3] In the months preceding the death march, two senior British officials had been murdered in Kabul, yet no action had been taken. Elphinstone's indecisiveness and ineptitude in dealing with reality was seen as compromising the effectiveness of the entire army. The massacre was a huge defeat for the British forces.[4]

Both these military examples illustrate the necessity of keeping a proper balance between *reality* and *hope*. In life, we too are sometimes caught in difficult situations where we are tempted to go to the extreme in our reactions and subsequently, we lose our ability to view things objectively. On the one hand we can become overwhelmed with negative or seemingly unchangeable circumstances, eventually causing us to lose hope. On the other hand, as illustrated by these military battles, we can be naïve or overly optimistic or even intentionally choose to ignore facts that are irrefutable. Either way, we are refusing to properly deal with reality. Neither response is correct. And as we will see in our study, neither are they biblical.

## UNDERSTANDING OUR TERMS

The word *reality* can conjure up a great many things in our minds, but in its most basic form it refers to what is *real* or *actual*, something that exists independently of any speculation. Many entities can be said to be real: things, facts, events, people.[5] Reality is simply what *is*.

On the other hand, hope may or may not deal with something that exists at this specific moment. In the dictionary, hope is defined as "the feeling that what is wanted can be had or that events will turn out for the best." The verb form of *hope* means "to look forward to something with desire and reasonable confidence; to feel that something desired may happen; or to believe, desire, or trust."[6]

As we saw in chapter 5, *biblical* hope must be understood differently from the world's concept of hope. There is always a significant measure of doubt in the world's hope; what is hoped for may come to pass—or it may not.

But the hope of God's Word is not like that. This hope is consistently described in Scripture as an absolute certainty that can be depended upon (Colossians 1:27; Galatians 5:5; Hebrews 11:1). As Alistair Begg explains:

> [T]he New Testament, when it uses the word "hope," knows nothing of uncertainty...To know this hope is to know the assurance of a reality that you have not yet fully experienced. It is not something that is in doubt. It is something that has been promised by the God of truth. It is a secure hope. It is a hope that breeds confidence. It is a hope based on the knowledge that "those whom he foreknew he also predestined to be conformed to the image of his Son" (Romans 8:29), and he "who began a good work in you will bring it to completion" (Philippians 1:6).[7]

In our normal usage of these words, however, reality stands in sharp contrast to the wishful or speculative hope of the world. Being realistic relies on thinking and evaluation since these are essential if we are to view a situation objectively. Reality requires us to carefully analyze all the contributing factors, both past and present. What are the overall positives and negatives? What motives and goals are in operation here, good or bad? What are the probable outcomes of certain actions? What are the potential ramifications for the individuals in this particular set of circumstances? Seeing the true situation can require a significant amount of thought and time, and even then we can't be sure we understand completely. It's always possible there are factors we have not taken into account. The best we can do is assess all aspects of a situation as accurately and dispassionately as possible and then try to respond appropriately.

Hope, on the other hand, is generally associated with concepts such as having faith and believing the best, both about circumstances and people. Hope is optimistic. It focuses its time and attention on the firm belief that people can change and situations can improve. When there is uncertainty, rather than automatically thinking the worst, this hopeful perspective gives people the benefit of the doubt. Hope is predisposed to view the glass as half-full while the tendency of reality can be to see it as half-empty. It is easy, then, to recognize the disparity in these two perspectives and the need for an equitable balance.

## TIMELESS CASE STUDIES
### Joseph's Life of Many Colors
As always, the Word of God stands ready to help us navigate through these issues. Scripture provides us with helpful examples portraying a harsh reality that was covered and redeemed by hope. One of the first instances we find is from the life of Joseph in the book of Genesis. To say that Joseph had experienced hardship in his life is an understatement. As a young man, his father, Jacob, unwisely showed him favoritism, with Joseph's "robe of many colors" being one of many things that made his siblings resent him (Genesis 37:3). Because of their growing jealousy, eventually Joseph was callously sold into slavery by his own brothers and taken away to a foreign land. He was then falsely accused by a devious woman and thrown into an Egyptian prison for a number of years. Yet in

Genesis 50:20, as Joseph's contrite brothers seek his forgiveness after their father's death, we hear him speak these astounding words: "As for you, you meant evil against me; but God meant it for good, to bring it about that many people should be kept alive, as they are today."

Joseph's reality had indeed been one of suffering and abuse; his trials, though, had humbled and refined him through the years and had enabled him to see the greater purposes of God being worked out in his life. There is no question that his brothers did intend evil against him. After his years in prison, however, Joseph miraculously gained the favor of Pharaoh and was promoted to the second highest office in Egypt and given the responsibility of steering the country through a terrible famine. The wicked actions of his brothers ultimately resulted in Joseph's ability to not only provide food for Egypt but for his own family as well. When Joseph was cruelly thrown into a pit by his brothers, who could possibly have foreseen God's amazing plan?

### A Desperate Cry for Help

In 2 Chronicles 20, we find the gripping story of King Jehoshaphat of Judah. His painful reality was that he felt totally helpless in the face of the enemy armies that were threatening to destroy him and his people. In response to this emergency, he took wise and appropriate action. The king led the entire nation to seek the Lord in fasting and prayer, appealing to God for mercy, and ending with Jehoshaphat's heartfelt confession that "we are powerless before this great multitude who are coming against us; nor do we know what to do, but our eyes are on You" (20:12).

The Lord heard their cry and fought for them, miraculously saving them from their enemies. This is a chapter for those who are without hope; we can learn much from Jehoshaphat's example of humbly depending on God and looking to Him for deliverance.

### The "Real" Reality

Another example of the contrast between reality and hope is found in one of my favorite stories in the Old Testament. We read this account in 2 Kings 6:8-17, which concerns the prophet Elisha. In this narrative, the king of Syria was greatly incensed because God had more than once revealed Syria's battle plans to Elisha, who in turn had warned the king of Israel so that he could fortify the cities about to be attacked. The king of Syria initially thought he had a traitor in his own household. But when he was told that Elisha was the informant, the king sent a great army to capture the prophet. In the middle of the night, all his horses and chariots and Syrian troops surrounded the town of Dothan where Elisha was staying. When Elisha's servant woke up early and saw the army encompassing the city, he ran to the prophet, frantic and fearful for their lives: "Alas, my Master! What shall we do?" (v. 15) But Elisha, the man of God, was cool and calm; he knew his Lord well, as revealed by his confident statement, "Do not be afraid, for those who are with us are more than those who are with them" (v. 16). The narrative continues, "Then Elisha prayed and said, 'O LORD, please open his eyes that he may see.' So the LORD opened the eyes of the young man, and he saw, and behold, the mountain was full of horses and chariots of fire all around Elisha" (v.

17). During the night, unbeknownst to the servant, God had sent His heavenly host to protect them from the Syrian army—but the servant was blind to it until the Lord spiritually opened his eyes.

Elisha's servant thought he was being realistic in this situation—and he was. There is no doubt that the Syrian army was there. But what the servant could not see was the *real* reality: God was there too! It's very easy to lose our perspective when we are in difficult circumstances. We can be so overwhelmed with the reality we *see* that we are blind to the reality that we *can't* see. Never forget, as explained in chapter 5, that there are two kingdoms in this world, the temporal and the eternal. We must guard against getting so caught up in the temporal that we lose sight of the eternal dimensions of our lives.

### King David: Delivered from His Dilemmas

In the life of King David, we find more illustrations of the important balance between reality and hope. David frequently found himself in challenging predicaments. Some resulted from the wicked actions of other people, but sadly, many were of his own making. In Psalm 3, we see him fleeing from his son Absalom, who was seeking to disgrace his father and steal the kingdom from him. In the beginning verses of Psalm 3, David is being brutally honest about his situation:

> O Lord, how many are my foes! Many are rising against me; many are saying of my soul, "There is no salvation for him in God." (3:1-2)

He saw clearly how dire his predicament was. It seemed hopeless; many had turned against him and joined Absalom's rebellion and were now seeking to kill him. David was being completely realistic about his dangerous situation. Yet surprisingly, as the psalm continues, we hear these words:

> But you, O LORD, are a shield about me, my glory, and the lifter of my head. I cried aloud to the LORD, and he answered me from his holy hill...I lay down and slept; I woke again, for the LORD sustained me. I will not be afraid of many thousands of people who have set themselves against me all around...For you strike all my enemies on the cheek; you break the teeth of the wicked. Salvation belongs to the LORD; your blessing be on your people! Selah. (3:3-8)

What had changed? Had Absalom been defeated? Had David been restored to his throne? No, his reality had not changed at all. He was still fleeing for his life from his own son. But what *had* been altered was his outlook on his circumstances. We are given another illustration of this dynamic in Psalm 13, where we once again see a dramatic shift take place between the first verse and the last:

> How long, O LORD? Will you forget me forever? How long will you hide your face from me? How long must I take counsel in my soul and have sorrow in my heart all the day? How long shall my enemy be exalted over me? Consider and answer

me, O LORD my God; light up my eyes, lest I sleep the sleep of death, lest my enemy say, "I have prevailed over him," lest my foes rejoice because I am shaken. But I have trusted in your steadfast love; my heart shall rejoice in your salvation. I will sing to the LORD, because he has dealt bountifully with me. (13:1-6)

In both these psalms, we find David fervently crying for help and almost despairing in the opening verses; yet by the end, he is singing and thanking and praising God! A number of David's other psalms show this same pattern of moving from despair to hope. Psalms 5, 7, 55, 57, 59, and 140 are just a few. As we study these, it becomes clear that in the course of his sometimes-turbulent life, David had learned to find the balance between reality and hope.

As we trace his transformation in these particular psalms, David gives us several clues as to what had revolutionized his thinking. He repeatedly acknowledges that his voice and his prayers had been heard by the Lord (Psalm 3:4; 5:3; 55:17,19). He recalls how the Lord had saved and protected in the past (Psalm 3:3,8; 55:16,22; 59:16; 140:12). He reminds himself of God's power and complete sovereignty over the entire universe (Psalm 7:8-9; 57:2-3; 59:5,13). Lastly, David focuses his mind on essential attributes of God such as righteousness (Psalm 5:4; 7:9,17); loving-kindness (Psalm 5:7,12; 57:10; 59:10,17); and immutability (Psalm 55:19). All these things that he knew to be true lifted him above his current reality and guided him back towards hope.

*Every Situation Is a Sovereign Situation*

Moving on to the New Testament, we see this critical balance again. Romans 8:28 is such an oft-quoted verse that we must be careful not to take for granted the profound, far-reaching truth it conveys:

> And we know that for those who love God all things work together for good, for those who are called according to his purpose.

As has been frequently pointed out, this verse does not say that all things are good; it says that all things *work* for good in the lives of God's children. That is a crucial distinction. And here is where harsh reality often crashes into the picture. Many times our reality is *not* good. Life's realities can run the gamut from being simply frustrating to being unspeakably painful or even catastrophic. Yet this verse makes no exceptions. No matter how distressing our situation, the Lord gives us His promise that He will *always* use it for His glory and our good. We may not like it; we may not understand it; we very likely would not have chosen it. But none of those things change the fact that God has allowed it and it is being used for His purposes. To know this and believe it is to take a monumental step in the direction of hope.

Romans 8:28 ushers us into the vast doctrine of the sovereignty of God, a subject that we will briefly examine here and revisit in the next chapter. If hope were a building, the sovereignty of God would be the foundation. If hope were a sailing ship, God's wise providence would be the wind that directs it. Recognizing that every molecule in the universe is under God's control and having the assurance that *everything* will be used for our good is what ultimately enables us to reach out and hold onto hope with both hands. How can we not acknowledge the presence of hope when we know our omniscient, omnipotent God is at work? In our times of greatest struggle and difficulty, these are timeless truths we must cling to if we are to stay balanced.

### Paul's Perspective

The apostle Paul, like Joseph and David, certainly did not lack for painful circumstances in his life. He had personal experience with the "all things" he referred to in Romans 8:28. In 2 Corinthians 11:23-28, we find a staggering list of all the beatings, imprisonments, and shipwrecks that he survived, along with a description of the abuses and dangers of every kind that he had endured. If anyone ever had reason to break under the sheer weight of reality and lose hope, it was Paul. Yet in 2 Corinthians 4:8-9, he declares: "We are afflicted in every way, but not crushed; perplexed, but not driven to despair; persecuted, but not forsaken; struck down, but not destroyed." Later in that same book he testifies that he is "sorrowful, yet always rejoicing...having nothing, yet possessing every-thing" (6:10). Paul knew well the sufficiency of his Lord (Romans 8:28; 2 Corinthians 12:9-10); thus he too had learned how to deal with the harshest of realities and yet keep his firm grip on hope.

## RESTING IN HIS SOVEREIGNTY

So here is the obvious question: how do we become this type of person? How do we remain steady and unshaken when the bitter winds of reality are blowing with all their might against our faith? We are told in Matthew 7:24-27 about the house built on the rock and the house built on the sand. How do we build a house that will stand strong in the fiercest storm? As we saw earlier, King David has much to teach us here. In his darkest times, he remembered that God heard his prayers; he recalled how the Lord had delivered him in the past; he acknowledged the utter sovereignty of God, not only over his own life but over the whole of creation; and he continually meditated on the character of God. All these responses are vital, but I want to specifically focus on both God's sovereignty and God's character as it relates to balancing reality with hope.

Scripture repeatedly attests to the doctrine of the sovereignty of God (Genesis 50:20; Psalm 103:19; 115:3; Job 42:2; Isaiah 14:24,26-27; 46:9-10; Daniel 4:35; Ephesians 1:11; Colossians 1:16). When we are struggling with our situation, it is imperative that we remember God's sovereignty over the most minuscule details of our lives. We must understand that "it is not outward circumstances that can drag us down, but our own reaction of despair to them, *when we fail to perceive the hidden hand of God in all events.*"[8] (emphasis added) The Lord is continually at work, even when we cannot comprehend what He's doing. And because of this truth, we must also be on guard against complaining. We must come to the realization that if God is truly sovereign, then all of our complaints are ultimately against *Him* and whatever He has permitted in our lives. As challenging as it might be, many of His highest purposes for us are accomplished not through eliminating a difficult reality but through allowing it to persist. Isaiah reminds us that God's thoughts are not our thoughts and His ways are not our ways; instead, they are infinitely higher (Isaiah 55:8-9). Martyn Lloyd-Jones reflects on these verses:

> [I]n the things that happen to us, our thinking is prone to become rational thinking again, and we must not be surprised therefore if we do not understand God's ways, for they are altogether different from ours. The difference between the two outlooks is the difference between heaven and earth.[9]

We must recognize that the trials and suffering that are sometimes part of our reality are serving good and indispensable purposes. First of all, they humble us and tend to get our attention as nothing else will. They drive us to God. As C.S. Lewis has famously stated, "God whispers to us in our pleasures, speaks in our conscience, but shouts in our pains."[10] Elisabeth Elliot's words ring true when she says, "The deepest things that I have learned in my own life have come from the deepest suffering. And out of the deepest waters and the hottest fires have come the deepest things that I know about God."[11] Psalm 119 teaches us that affliction also opens our ears to hear God's Word:

> Before I was afflicted I went astray, but now I keep your word....It is good for me that I was afflicted, that I might learn your statutes. (119:67,71)

Realizing that our suffering, then, is somehow being used for our good enables us to have hope—hope that we are growing in our love for God and His Word, hope that our character is becoming more Christlike. In fact, this is the "good" that is referred to in Romans 8:28-29—our good is not comfort or happiness or material blessings but that we would be more conformed to the image of Jesus Christ:

> And we know that for those who love God all things work together for good, for those who are the called according to his purpose. For those whom he foreknew he also predestined to be conformed to the image of his Son.

This is why the doctrine of the sovereignty of God should bring such comfort and hope—He is using *every* situation in our lives, both good and bad, to make us more like Jesus. We live in a sinful, fallen world, but there are no accidents in this life for those who belong to Christ. If we thought all the heartaches of our lives were simply random accidents, totally disconnected from God and out of His control, this would surely lead us to despair. But knowing that our loving Father is sovereignly working in our lives for good makes a monumental difference in how we view our particular reality.

## CLINGING TO HIS CHARACTER

Here is another key: we must hold tightly to the character of God, especially when we are in great distress and struggling to make sense of what He's doing in our lives. Taking time to meditate on His attributes will bring encouragement to our hearts. His perfections are truly beyond our comprehension, yet He allows us to know a measure of them in order to bring us comfort and assurance, as well as to bring us to worship. For example, He is eternally self-existent and self-sufficient (Genesis 1:1; John 1:1; 5:26). He is immutable (Psalm 102:27; Malachi 3:6; Hebrews 13:8; James 1:17). He is holy and righteous and faithful (Ezekiel 39:7; Psalm 11:7; 33:4). He is a transcendent God who has all wisdom and all power over the entire universe (1 Chronicles 29:10-12; Psalm 145:3-6; Isaiah 40:26,28; 57:15), and He is simultaneously an immanent Father who condescends to show us love, grace, and tender mercy (Psalm 34:17-19; 145:8-9,14,18-19). He is a God of justice and wrath (Psalm 89:14; 103:6; Romans 1:18) and we can trust, therefore, that someday every wrong will be made right. He is in all things a *good* God (Psalm 34:8; 107:1; 119:68) and in this we find profound hope. Mary Mohler talks about the importance of focusing on the attributes of God and being grateful for who He is:

> I am talking about a deep sense of awe ingrained in our minds. I am talking about an awareness, in every waking moment, of the glorious truth that the God of the universe is infinite in all his perfections. And he loves us.[12]

Elliot also testifies to the peace that is ours when we grasp the fact that God loves us and is actively guiding our lives:

> And that's what Christianity is about. God is God. God is a three-personed God. He loves us. We are

not adrift in chaos. To me that is the most forti-
fying, the most stabilizing, the most peace-giving
thing that I know anything about in the universe.
Every time things have seemingly fallen apart in
my life I have gone back to those things that do not
change. Nothing in the universe can ever change
those facts. He loves me. I am not at the mercy of
chance.[13]

### Our Sovereign Is Our Savior

As we focus here on the importance of God's character, we find helpful insight in the book of Lamentations.
Penned by the weeping prophet Jeremiah, Lamentations
3:21-22 is a familiar Bible passage because of its enduring
encouragement: "The steadfast love of the LORD never
ceases; his mercies never come to an end; they are new
every morning; great is your faithfulness." But for those
who are not familiar with the whole of Lamentations 3,
the first twenty verses may actually come as a bit of a
shock.

The opening portion of this chapter is a dark reality
indeed; here we witness Jeremiah sharing the sufferings
of the nation of Israel. He is pictured as a man trapped in
a hopeless situation from which there is no escape. Every
cry for help is shut out; every attempt to escape is blocked;
words like *bitterness* and *hardship* reveal the despondent state
of his heart. Jeremiah is in utter despair and finally brings
his lament to a close with these tragic, heart-wrenching
words: "My soul has been rejected from peace; I have forgotten happiness. So I say, 'My strength has perished, And
so has my hope from the LORD'" (vv.17-18, NASB). He

has lost hope. But what makes this passage so intriguing is that all this terrible affliction is not attributed to random providence but to a *person*. From the very beginning, we find masculine pronouns in almost every verse: "He has broken my bones (v.4); He has blocked my ways (v.9); He has...torn me to pieces; He has made me desolate (v.11). Jeremiah fully understood that the author of his pain and misery was *God*.

But like a drowning man gasping for oxygen, Jeremiah desperately fights his way up, up, up, to the surface of his suffering. And in verse 21, we see him finally break through and get his first gulp of life-giving air that is contained in those beautiful words: "The steadfast love of the Lord never ceases." From verses 21 through 40, we then find Jeremiah with a totally different outlook as he extols the lovingkindness, mercy, faithfulness, and goodness of the Lord. Three times, in verses 21, 24, and 29, we hear him expressing hope. Even more important, all these qualities are found *in* the Lord: "'The Lord is my portion,' says my soul, 'therefore I have hope in Him'" (v.24); "The Lord is good to those who wait for Him, to the person who seeks Him" (v.25). Jeremiah was clearly not finding his comfort in material blessings but in the *person* of God.

But wait—isn't this the same God who was oppressing him so sorely in the first twenty verses? Has Jeremiah simply forgotten about the terrible torment he had endured at God's hands? We see pictured here an amazing spiritual paradox, that He who is ultimately responsible for our suffering is also responsible for our salvation; He who has sovereignly allowed our distress is also the supreme source of our hope.

As believers, we don't like the thought that a good God would have anything to do with our trials. We want to "protect" Him and effectively disconnect Him from all our maladies—and yet Scripture itself steadfastly refuses to do that. What do we do with sobering and unsettling verses such as these?

> Then the LORD said to him, "Who has made man's mouth? Who makes him mute, or deaf, or seeing, or blind? Is it not I, the LORD?" (Exodus 4:11)

> I form light and create darkness; I make well-being and create calamity; I am the LORD, who does all these things. (Isaiah 45:7)

> …Does disaster come to a city, unless the LORD has done it? (Amos 3:6)

> I kill and I make alive; I wound and I heal; and there is none that can deliver out of my hand. (Deuteronomy 32:39)

Lamentations 3 further instructs us that nothing can come to pass unless God commands it and it is "from the mouth of the Most High that good and bad come" (3:37-38). In 1 Samuel 2:6-7, we are again told: "The LORD kills and brings to life…The LORD makes poor and makes rich."

In the book of Job, Job's admonition to his wife indicates that he well understood this truth about the Lord's sovereignty over everything, both good *and* bad, that touched his life: "Shall we indeed accept good from God, and not accept adversity?" (Job 2:10, NASB) Later on, as Job muses on God's loving discipline, we also hear these thought-provoking words: "For he wounds, but he binds up; he shatters, but his hands heal." (5:18)

The inescapable biblical truth is that God has *everything* to do with our circumstances. He is utterly sovereign, and nothing can afflict us without His divine action or permission. Yet the age-old problem is that our limited human understanding struggles greatly to reconcile a loving God with the suffering that exists in our lives.

We find the enigma of Lamentations 3 pictured elsewhere in Scripture. In Psalm 38:2, as David voices his laments, he refers specifically to "*Your* arrows" and "*Your* hand." Then we turn to Psalm 42, where the opening verses reveal the psalmist passionately panting and thirsting for God. But as the psalm continues and he begins to acknowledge the difficulties in his life, he addresses the Lord directly, crying out: "Your breakers and Your waves have rolled over me" (42:7, NASB). It is significant that he does not call them "*the* breakers" and "*the* waves." He is clearly confessing his awareness that these are not random acts but instead, it is *the Lord* who has intentionally allowed these troubles in his life—and yet in the end, the psalmist's all-consuming desire is simply to be in the presence of the very One who has permitted his suffering.

How can we explain this paradox except by seeing in it our *complete trust* in the character of God? In our next chapter, we will look at this issue in more detail. Yes, God is my Sovereign King who controls every detail of the universe. He is, however, not only my Sovereign, He is also my Savior who died for me and my loving Father whom I trust. He is my Strength, my Rock, my Fortress, my Deliverer, my Refuge, my Stronghold (Psalm 18:1-2). He is the good Shepherd who tenderly leads me and laid down His life for me (Psalm 23; John 10:11,14-15). And because of this assurance of the *goodness* of God, even though I may not always understand His mysterious and sometimes painful providence in my life, I choose to believe that ultimately, it is for my best. I desperately need His love, His guidance, and His grace, especially in my times of difficulty; therefore, just like David and Jeremiah, even as I see His hand in all my circumstances, I will desire Him *more*, not less.

In summary, these are just a few of the keys that will enable us to keep our ships steady in the storms of life and navigate surely in this narrow strait between reality and hope. We must fix our eyes firmly on God's character; we must believe that the purpose of His sovereignty is always our good and His glory; and we must remind ourselves that He hears our prayers and has always been faithful to guide us in the past.

## DON'T FORGET THE BASICS

We cannot forget that regularly spending time in Bible study and in prayer must undergird everything else we may do. How will we ever know who God is if we don't spend time in His Word? How will we ever know that He hears our prayers if we never pray? All of our spiritual endeavors need to be intertwined with the careful study of God's Word and a faithful prayer life. Sinclair Ferguson comments on the necessity of being a diligent student of Scripture:

> Listening submissively to the voice of God is what brings us the knowledge of God...It is in scripture we learn how God views himself, ourselves, and the world, and what he wants us to know in order to serve him...In growing to know God, therefore, there is no substitute for the discipline of Bible study and Scripture reading and meditation. We cannot bypass the handbook that God has given to us and then expect that we can know him in our own way.[14]

Eric Alexander stresses the priority of prayer by reminding us that "throughout the Bible, prayer is fundamental and not supplemental in the personal and corporate lives of God's people."[15]

J. C. Ryle makes the point that prayer is an indispensable part of what it means to be a child of God:

> The first act of faith will be to speak to God...Prayer is to faith what breath is to life. How a man can live and not breathe is past my comprehension, and how a man can believe and not pray is past my comprehension too.[16]

It is therefore of first importance that we not neglect the nurture of these vital disciplines in our lives. Our stability and spiritual growth depend upon them.

## REALITY UNOPPOSED

We have seen that we need to maintain a balanced perspective in our life circumstances—but what happens when we feel our boats listing to one side or another in any particular storm? What does it look like when we have been swamped by wave after wave of overwhelming reality and begin to be knocked off balance? Since this is a broken, sinful world, we should not be surprised if over time we may be repeatedly disappointed by other people. Situations and circumstances may grow increasingly difficult and stressful and they begin to take a toll on our outlook and ability to persevere. One of the first symptoms that we may detect in our hearts is a growing tendency toward skepticism and cynicism. When we have been hurt and disillusioned by either people or events we've experienced, our tendency is to become self-protective in order to avoid being hurt again. Our disillusionment can subtly transition to an increasingly cynical, pessimistic attitude toward life in general, and we can begin to be distrustful of other people and their intentions. If there is no balancing element of hopefulness, this can further degenerate into a simmering bitterness that takes root in our souls. Sadly, for many, despair and depression are waiting at the end of this dark and dangerous road.

It is imperative, if this is your bent, to consciously fix your mind on the hope that is abundant in Scripture. Stay in God's Word, earnestly seek the Holy Spirit's help, and enlist the prayer support of your Christian sisters and brothers for your struggles. Deliberately and steadfastly refuse to listen to the lies of Satan and the hopeless whispers of a lost world. Fight for hope! John Piper counsels us here:

> Despair is relentless in the certainties of its pessimism. But we have seen again and again...that absolute statements of hopelessness that we make in the dark are notoriously unreliable. Our dark certainties are not sureties. While we have the light, let us cultivate distrust of the certainties of despair.[17]

## FOOLISH HOPE

What of the other extreme, the person who tends to err on the side of hope to the point of becoming illogical, unreasonable, or even irrational? What of the person who steadfastly refuses to evaluate situations honestly and deal with reality? This can also be damaging because the end result is that nothing is ever improved or resolved. Especially when we are dealing with sin in another person's life, there are times when we must be honest and forthright about our concerns. Even if it is not a true sin issue, to be naïve and willfully close our eyes to thinking and behavior that is unprofitable is not loving. As we saw in chapter 4, sometimes we refuse to speak or confront because we're afraid of the personal cost to ourselves. But to be foolishly optimistic to the point of denying facts and completely ignoring reality is not helpful to anyone. There are times when the most loving thing we can do for someone we care for is to gently tell them the truth. We must always be gracious but honest. It is ultimately a sign of immaturity to ignore the facts and instead choose to live in a fantasy world that refuses to come to terms with real life. These type of people do not solve problems but simply look the other way. They too must earnestly seek the counsel of the Word and fellow believers and pray the Spirit will grant them wisdom, discernment, and boldness to accurately evaluate their life situations.

## HOLDING ONTO BOTH

One of the crucial tasks, then, of the Christian life is to learn how to hold onto reality and hope at the same time. We must be ever hopeful but must also objectively acknowledge the reality of our situation and the Lord's sovereignty over all our circumstances. We could label this balance "realistic optimism" or perhaps "optimistic real-ism." It simply means that no matter how bad our situation might appear, we must trust that our God is continually working out His divine and mysterious purposes in our lives. He is sovereign; He is all-wise and all-powerful; He is the heart-changer; He is the One who unfailingly brings good out of bad; and most of all, He loves us with a love that is beyond comprehension. There is *always* hope if we are God's children; to say there is no hope is to attack the very character of God—because He *is* the God of hope.

We find so many verses about hope in Scripture. We are called to hope (Ephesians 1:18). We hope in His Word (Psalm 119:74,81); we hope in His mercy (Psalm 33:18); we hope for His salvation (Psalm 119:166; Lamentations 3:26); and we have the hope of eternal life (Colossians 1:5; Titus 1:2; 3:7). Most of all, we hope in *Him* (Psalm 31:24; 38:15; 42:5; 71:5; 146:5; 1 Timothy 1:1; Titus 2:13; 1 Peter 1:21). We hope for what we do not see (Romans 8:24-25;

Hebrews 11:1) and as Hebrews 6:19 tells us, this hope is the very anchor of our souls. We *never* stop hoping (Psalm 71:14). It is clear from God's Word that His purpose for His children is that we would overflow with hope:

> For whatever was written in former days was written for our instruction, that through endurance and through the encouragement of the Scriptures we might have hope...May the God of hope fill you with all joy and peace in believing, so that by the power of the Holy Spirit you may abound in hope. (Romans 15:4,13)

Begg summarizes the glorious hope we have in Christ and the difference it makes in the way we live our lives:

> In this certain hope lies the Christian's hope and confidence and excitement. We know our best days are all ahead of us. We know that death is not the end of the best time of our life; it's the start of it. That's hard to remember. That's hard to cling onto in a world that's hopeless and in circumstances that can sometimes look hopeless...That's why you need to ask God to make your hope real to you, and ask God to make it real to those around you. Pray for a focus on your hope.[18]

## PORTRAITS OF REALITY AND HOPE

This topic has led me to ponder the lives of Christians who have embodied this important balance. In each of their lives, *hope* has more than held its own with *reality*.

Fanny Crosby's reality was that she lost her sight as an infant and lived her entire life as a blind woman. Yet she became a famous poet and composer, writing over 8,000 hymns and gospel songs, many of which are still sung today. We marvel at the hopeful, thankful perspective she revealed in these amazing words: "It seemed intended by the blessed providence of God that I should be blind all my life, and I thank him for the dispensation. If perfect earthly sight were offered me tomorrow I would not accept it. I might not have sung hymns to the praise of God if I had been distracted by the beautiful and interesting things about me."[19]

Susannah Spurgeon, wife of Charles Spurgeon, dealt with serious health issues most of her adult life that basically left her an invalid for many years. Yet she refused to give up hope and focus on herself and her problems. Instead she remained a faithful pastor's wife, supporting her husband's ministry, raising two sons, and starting and maintaining a book fund for pastors who could not afford to buy them. By the time of her death, her book fund had provided over 200,000 volumes free of charge to pastors. She wrote several devotional books and also contributed to a biography of Charles after his death in 1892.[20] She refused to allow her physical suffering to destroy her hope and her effectiveness in the work of the kingdom.

George Washington Carver was born into slavery in the 1860s and eventually committed his life to Christ. Although he experienced terrible racial injustice in his lifetime, he pursued his education diligently and established a reputation as a brilliant botanist and inventor. Embarking on a stellar career of teaching and research at the Tuskegee Institute in Alabama, he achieved national prominence and influence. He devoted his life to impacting others for good with his groundbreaking research and intentionally based his approach on biblical principles. He never allowed his reality to overcome him but instead gave clear testimony of hope and faith and lived his life for God's glory.[21]

In 1955, Jim Elliot and four other missionaries were brutally murdered in Ecuador by the native people they were trying to evangelize, leaving several young wives grieving and alone—a harsh reality indeed. Yet those they left behind grounded their hope in the sovereignty of a loving God. The well-known story of the martyrdom of these five men has had an incalculable effect on Christendom, inspiring an untold number of individuals to dedicate their lives to full-time Christian service. In particular, Jim's widow, Elisabeth, had a long and fruitful ministry as an author and conference speaker who gave powerful testimony to the faithfulness of God. Her reality did not override her hope.

We have many current day examples of this balance to also encourage us. Joni Eareckson Tada has been a quadriplegic since a diving accident in 1967. This is an all-consuming reality that very few people will ever have to deal with in life. Yet in spite of this hardship, Joni has been an incredible inspiration to countless people as she lives out her faith and hope in her Savior alongside her husband Ken. She is a talented artist, a well-known author, a singer, a radio host, and a conference speaker. In 1979, she founded a ministry called Joni and Friends that today ministers in a multitude of ways to people with physical challenges all over the world.[22]

In 2008, at the age of twenty-six, Katherine Wolf experienced a massive brain stem stroke that almost took her life. She miraculously survived and despite her continuing physical effects from the stroke, she and her husband started a ministry to disabled individuals and their families. She is an author and conference speaker and brings her message of hope to many.[23] Fittingly enough, Katherine and Jay's ministry is called "Hope Heals," and I can't think of a better name. Hope, biblical hope, hope in Jesus Christ *does* heal; most important of all, it heals our souls and gives us the power and the ability to deal with difficult realities in our lives.

## THE EXTREMES

When we get out of balance, then, in this area of reality and hope, what does it look like? What are the symptoms that can begin to surface in our lives? If you are excessive in your emphasis on *reality*, this is what you may see:

- Skepticism/cynicism/pessimism
- Bitterness
- Despair/depression

If you are too extreme on the side of *hope*, here are the possible symptoms:

- Naivete
- Foolish or unreasonable optimism
- Immature refusal to deal with reality

## HOPE THAT IS REAL

As that great hymn reminds us, "in Christ alone" our hope is found.[24] In contrast to the reality of this world, our hope that is grounded in God becomes its *own* reality. It is a hope based on absolute truth and therefore we can trust it. It is the "real" reality! The unassailable reason we have hope—and always will—is because we have a *good* God who loves us, no matter what our circumstances. We are reminded of this in 2 Samuel:

> And now, O Lord GOD, You are God, and Your words are true, and You have promised this goodness to Your servant. (7:28, NKJV)

We find these same thoughts beautifully expressed in the final stanzas of this song:

> Come and find our hope now in Jesus
> He is all He said He would be
> Grace is overflowing from the Savior's heart
> Rest here in His wondrous peace
>
> Oh the Goodness, the Goodness of Jesus
> Satisfied He is all that I need
> May it be, come what may, that I rest all my days
> In the Goodness of Jesus[25]

## *For Personal Reflection and Application*

### CHAPTER 7—REALITY AND HOPE

1.  Read Genesis 45:3-8. What is the natural sinful reaction to being sinned against by others? What did Joseph know about God that gave him the ability to respond to his brothers as he did in Genesis 50:20? Have you ever been wronged? How did you respond? What did you learn through that experience?

2.  Read through Psalm 3 and describe David's difficult situation. What did he declare about the Lord in this psalm and how did this knowledge give him hope? What are some of the truths about God that personally give you hope?

3.  Study Romans 12:17-21. Can you remember an example of when you were able to overcome evil with good? Is there a current situation in your life where you need to apply this principle?

4.  The apostle Paul endured great difficulties in his life, yet he found great hope in his Lord. Read through these passages and give your thoughts on what he had learned about God that enabled him to endure. (1 Corinthians 2:4-5; 2 Corinthians 1:8-10; 12:9-10; Ephesians 3:16-20)

5. The spiritual disciplines of Bible study and prayer are essential to maintaining hope in the midst of our trials. Share some of the scriptures that have encouraged you the most in times of suffering. How does bringing your burdens to the Lord in prayer give you hope?

6. Romans 8:28 promises us that God sovereignly works for our good in all circumstances. What does verse 29 tell us about His ultimate purpose for us? Think back to a situation you have faced where you did not see how any good could come from it. Share the beneficial results that you are now able to see from that situation.

# ENDNOTES

1 History. (2009). "Battle of the Bulge." *History.com* (October 14). https://www.history.com/topics/world-war-ii/battle-of-the-bulge. Accessed June 24, 2020.

2 Wikipedia. (2020). "Battle of the Bulge." https://en.wikipedia.org/wiki/Battle_of_the_Bulge. Accessed June 24, 2020.

3 Vandepeer, C. (2019). "Self-Deception and the 'Conspiracy of Optimism.'" *War on the Rocks* (January 31, 2019). https://warontherocks.com/2019/01/self-deception-and-the-conspiracy-of-optimism.

4 Wikipedia. (2020). "1842 retreat from Kabul." https://en.wikipedia.org/wiki/1842_retreat_from_Kabul.

5 Dictionary.com. (2020). "reality." Dictionary.com based on the Random House Unabridged Dictionary. https://www.dictionary.com. Accessed June 19, 2020.

6 Ibid., "hope."

7 Begg, A. (2019). *Pray Big: Learn to Pray Like an Apostle* (The Good Book Company), 49.

8 Roberts, M. (1995). *The Thought of God* (Carlisle, PA: The Banner of Truth Trust), 7.

9   Lloyd-Jones, M. (1994). *Reflections: A Treasury of Daily Readings* (Grand Rapids, MI: Wm. B. Eerdmans Publishing Co.), 64.

10  Lewis, C. S. (1940). *The Problem of Pain* (reprinted 2001, San Francisco: HarperSanFrancisco), 91.

11  Elliot, E. (2019). *Suffering is Never for Nothing* (Nashville, TN: B&H Publishing Group), 9.

12  Mohler, M. (2018). *Growing in Gratitude* (Epsom, UK: The Good Book Company), 10-11.

13  Elliot. *Suffering is Never for Nothing*, 43.

14  Ferguson, S. (1987). *A Heart for God* (Carlisle, PA: The Banner of Truth Trust), 7–8.

15  Alexander, E. (2012). *Prayer: A Biblical Perspective* (Carlisle, PA: The Banner of Truth Trust), ix.

16  Ryle, J. C. (2004). *A Call to Prayer* (Carlisle, PA: The Banner of Truth Trust), 7.

17  Piper, J. (2006). *When the Darkness Will Not Lift* (Wheaton, IL: Crossway Books),42–43.

18  Begg, A. (2019). *Pray Big: Learn to Pray Like an Apostle* (The Good Book Company), 55.

19  "Fanny Crosby: America's Hymn Queen." *Glimpses of Christian History 198*, https://www.christianhistorytimeline.com/GLIMPSEF/Glimpses2/glimpses198.shtml.

20  Banner of Truth. "Susannah Spurgeon." https://banneroftruth.org/us/about/banner-authors/susannah-spurgeon/. Accessed June 6, 2020.

21  Perry, J. (1999). *Unshakeable Faith* (Sisters, OR: Multnomah Publishers, Inc.).

22  For more information, see www.joniandfriends.org.

23  For more information, see www.hopeheals.com.

24  Townend, S. and Getty, K. "In Christ Alone." Copyright © 2001 Thankyou Music (Adm. by CapitolCMGPublishing.com excl. UK & Europe, adm. by Integrity Music, part of the David C Cook family, songs@integritymusic.com)

25  Aghajanian, F., Druery, H., Farren, M., Maxwell, J., Robinson, J., and Thompson, R. (2018). "The Goodness of Jesus." http://www.cityalight.com/wp-content/uploads/2018/12/The-Goodness-of-Jesus-Lead-Sheet.pdf.

*Whatever your hand finds to do,*
*do it with your might…*
—Ecclesiastes 9:10

*For we are his workmanship, created*
*in Christ Jesus for good works…*
—Ephesians 2:10

*…I labor, striving according to His power,*
*which mightily works within me.*
—Colossians 1:29 (NASB)

*…fight the good fight…*
—1 Timothy 1:18 (NASB)

*Trust in him at all times, O people;*
*pour out your heart before him;*
*God is a refuge for us.*
—Psalm 62:8

*Trust in the LORD with all your heart, and*
*do not lean on your own understanding.*
—Proverbs 3:5

*Blessed is the man who trusts in the*
*LORD, whose trust is the LORD.*
—Jeremiah 17:7

Chapter 8
# STRIVING AND TRUSTING

My father was a civil engineering professor most of his adult life, but one of his additional passions was piloting small planes. When I was in elementary school, he obtained his flying license. This allowed him to periodically fly to various jobsites around Texas to work as a consulting engineer. From time to time, my dad would take my mother, my older sister, and me on one of these trips. In my eight-year-old mind, flying in a plane was probably the most exciting thing in the whole world, and I was young enough to have no thought whatsoever that there could be any risk or danger involved. I loved the loud noise and the dipping motion of the plane when we made a turn. I especially loved it when my dad would have me put my hands on the copilot controls and ask me to "help" him fly the plane!

As we would expect, all planes, from the small, private ones to the larger military or commercial types, must meet very detailed regulations. For example, the airport mechanics follow strict maintenance schedules. Regular equipment checks include careful examinations of engines, landing gear, control surfaces, and other key systems.[1]

In addition, pilots have their own set of responsibilities related to the safety of their passengers. Before taking the plane up in the air, they must go through a methodical process called a "preflight." This includes a thorough investigation of the current weather conditions along with any temporary flight restrictions. There is detailed paperwork that must be put in order. Finally, the pilot performs a meticulous exterior and interior evaluation. After this extensive process has confirmed that all systems are ready, the pilot can then taxi to the runway and await clearance for takeoff. But even then, a conscientious pilot will continue to be alert and verify key information throughout the duration of the flight.[2]

Of course, while mechanics and pilots do all they can to guarantee the safety of their passengers, we still understand that it is impossible to predict, or control, every single variable that might affect the plane. There comes a point at which every passenger must simply choose to trust that every reasonable precaution has been taken to ensure a safe flight. This is an essential step of faith if air travelers are to fly without fear or anxiety. As a young child flying with my dad, however, I wasn't relying on the equipment or the maintenance process or the safety checks. I simply assumed that everything had been taken care of. And that assumption was rooted in an unspoken reality that was infinitely more profound: my *father* was the pilot and I knew that so long as I was with *him*, I would be all right. It was thus my quiet trust in a loving father that completely swept away any fears I might have had.

This final chapter addresses a topic that touches every corner of our lives: the ongoing, ever-present battle between *striving*—doing all that we know to do—and simply *trusting*. Many times in life, we've done the research, sought counsel, searched the scriptures, and prayed. Yet our situation still has not changed. At that point we must trust that the Lord is moving in ways we cannot comprehend. But trusting still does not negate the fact that we are responsible to do what we can.

These are therefore the two sides of this weighty coin that we flip on a daily basis: the striving/action side and the trusting/waiting side. Let me make it clear that I am not referring to the topic of salvation here. We do not *strive* to be saved. Out of His immense and incomprehensible mercy, God regenerates us and brings us to repentant faith. Our salvation is all of grace. So when I say striving and trusting, what I am referring to is the balance between God's role and our role in our *sanctification* and how we live our lives on this earth.

In this chapter we will touch on some of the same issues that we previously addressed as we sought to balance reality and hope. But the focus here will be more specifically on the practical choices we make in life and the ongoing need to both strive and trust.

## NEHEMIAH'S WALL

An illustration of this complementary tension is found in the book of Nehemiah. Sadly, because of Israel's unfaithfulness to God, both the northern and the southern kingdoms had been conquered by other nations and the people carried away into captivity. Many years later (ca. 539 BC), the Persian king Cyrus, moved by the sovereign hand of God, decreed that the captive Jews could return to Jerusalem to rebuild the Temple and reestablish their national feasts and sacrifices. This decree prompted three separate returns of the exiles to their homeland. Nehemiah was the leader of the third return (ca. 445 BC), with the goal of rebuilding the walls of Jerusalem that had been destroyed by the Babylonians in 587–586 BC.

As soon as Nehemiah arrived in Jerusalem, he encountered opposition from Judah's enemies, who had no desire to see Jerusalem restored to prominence under the Jews.[3] In Nehemiah 4:8, we are told that these adversaries "all plotted together to come and fight against Jerusalem and to cause confusion in it." Nehemiah carefully evaluated the situation and acted wisely: "And we prayed to our God and set a guard as a protection against them day and night" (v. 9). Thus the first thing the Jews did was pray and seek God's divine help and protection. But that was not all they did. Nehemiah also positioned families at strategic places on the wall, arming them with swords, spears, and bows. In verse 14, we hear his pep talk to his fellow Jews: "Do not be afraid of them. Remember the Lord, who is great and awesome, and fight for your brothers, your sons, your daughters, your wives, and your homes." On the one hand, He was exhorting them to remember God's power and depend on Him. But on the other hand, they were also to fight with all their strength if anyone attacked the wall. Here is how it played out:

From that day on, half of my servants worked on construction, and half held the spears, shields, bows, and coats of mail. And the leaders stood behind the whole house of Judah, who were building on the wall. Those who carried burdens were loaded in such a way that each labored on the work with one hand and held his weapon with the other. (vv. 16-17)

Nehemiah definitely understood the balance between striving and trusting! In this situation, God had a role, and so did the people of Judah. The end result was that in spite of strong opposition, the wall of Jerusalem was rebuilt in fifty-two days—an amazing accomplishment.

## THE NEVER-ENDING TENSION

We see other examples of this balance in Psalms and Proverbs. Psalm 127:1 reminds us that "unless the Lord builds the house, those who build it labor in vain." We labor, yes—but our labor alone is not enough. We have responsibilities to fulfill—but God is still actively at work. The book of Proverbs points out that He "is a shield to those who walk uprightly" (2:7). We are to live holy lives and be people of integrity (Psalm 15:1-5; 2 Corinthians 1:12; Philippians 2:15) and the Lord promises that He will be our shield. Another passage in Proverbs illustrates this tension as well: "Trust in the LORD with all your heart, and do not lean on your own understanding. In all your ways acknowledge him, and he will make straight your paths" (3:5-6). We are called to trust Him and depend on Him, and He in turn will guide our paths. Our part— His part. Lastly, we find a related principle in Proverbs 21: "The horse is made ready for the day of battle, but the victory belongs to the LORD" (21:31). We definitely have a responsibility to wisely prepare for the future. Yet the results always lie in the hands of God.

The New Testament teaches these principles as well. In 1 Corinthians 3:6-7, the apostle Paul refers to the spiritual work that had been done in the church at Corinth. He summarizes this work by saying that he had "planted" and his fellow minister, Apollos, had "watered." Paul emphasizes, however, that ultimately it was God who gave the growth. Without question, we are to be faithful to proclaim the gospel, but we must never forget that only the Lord can grant saving faith and repentance to a spiritually dead soul. While God does not need us in this process, He nevertheless has chosen to work through human instruments and allow His children to participate in bringing the good news to others. Both human and divine roles are thus included in His perfect plan.

We see this balance again in Ephesians 2:10, which says we have been created for good works. As believers, we know that walking in good works should be a hallmark of our lives, and our task is to be faithful and obedient to perform them. But this verse makes it clear that we were first *His* workmanship; He created us in Christ Jesus for this purpose and prepared our works for us beforehand. His part—our part!

The book of Philippians also addresses this issue. In Philippians 2:12-13, Paul instructs us to "work out your own salvation" but then immediately reminds us that it is God who works *in* us. Later, in chapter 4, the apostle is discussing our need to pray. We are to resist the continual temptation to be anxious and instead come humbly to our Father in prayer. What is God's responsibility? When we strive to obey this directive, God gives us a promise that He will graciously guard our hearts and minds with His supernatural peace that is beyond our understanding (4:6-7).

One of the most straightforward depictions of the balance between God's work and ours is found in Colossians 1:29: "For this purpose also I labor, striving according to His power, which mightily works within me." Just like Paul, we *do* labor; we definitely do play a role. Yet if our goal is to glorify the Lord, all of our striving, all of our obedience, everything we do must be according to the power of the Holy Spirit who lives inside of us.

In 1 Timothy 6:11-12, Paul is giving Timothy rapid-fire commands—flee sin; pursue righteousness, godliness, faith, love, steadfastness, and gentleness; fight the good fight of faith. These are the kinds of directives we as believers are to obey. But then in verse 12, he also reminds us of God's involvement: "Take hold of the eternal life to which you were called." The reason we obey is because we have been called to eternal life by the Lord Jesus. That is *His* part, and it is what motivates and strengthens us to do *our* part and thus honor the commands of Scripture.

Our final example is found in James 4:13-15, which deals with our aspirations for the future. We may have all sorts of plans, but James gives us a sober reminder that we have no idea what tomorrow may bring. So instead of pridefully thinking we can do anything we want, it is wiser to say, "If the Lord wills, we will live and do this or that" (v. 15). God gives us much freedom in this temporal sphere to develop our God-given abilities and talents, to pursue our goals, and to endeavor to live an obedient, God-glorifying life. That is our responsibility; but the Lord is always overseeing and guiding our steps, and we must submit our plans to His wise and loving providence.

All these scriptures illustrate the tension between striving and trusting. The conclusion is that we are to put utmost effort into faithfully serving the Lord—while trusting Him every step along the way. Yet if we are honest, most would admit that what comes more naturally to our self-sufficient humanness is the striving aspect. In general, it is much easier to stay busy and *do* something rather than to simply wait and trust. This could be called the "Martha Syndrome."

In the gospel accounts of Jesus' life, we are introduced to Mary and her older sister, Martha. Along with their brother, Lazarus, they were close friends of Jesus. In Luke 10:38-42, we have the narrative of a particular visit that Jesus made to their home. As Martha busied herself serving, Mary simply positioned herself at the Lord's feet so she could listen to His words. This frustrated Martha to the point that she eventually confronted Jesus, in essence ordering Him to instruct her younger sister to help out. Martha's words are truly shocking because we know she was speaking to God Incarnate! Yet Jesus went right to the heart of the matter as He gently spoke these gracious words, "Martha, Martha, you are anxious and troubled about many things, but one thing is necessary. Mary has chosen the good portion, which will not be taken away from her" (vv. 41-42). Listen to Charles Spurgeon's observations on this story of Mary and Martha:

Her fault was not that she served…Let us do all that we possibly can…It was no fault of hers that she was busy preparing a feast for the Master…Her fault was that she grew "distracted with much serving," so that she forgot Him, and only remembered the service. She allowed service to override communion…We ought to be Mary and Martha in one: we should do much service and have much communion at the same time. For this we need great grace. It is easier to serve than to commune.[4]

Spurgeon understood that it is much easier to be a Martha than a Mary. Striving comes naturally to most of us; trusting does not. Because of this reality, let's now take a more extensive look at the challenging issue of trusting God.

## THE TRUSTWORTHINESS OF GOD

Trusting the Lord is essential because we live in a fallen world, and that means we will regularly be thrust into situations that are totally out of our control. If there's one thing we can be sure of in this life, it is that at one time or another we will all encounter trouble (Job 5:7). Life is hard. The human condition includes not only physical pain but mental and emotional pain as well: the sharp sting of regret; the sorrow of lost opportunities and unrealized dreams; the sadness of loss and death. It is noteworthy that James said, "*when* you encounter various trials," not "if" (James 1:2, NASB, emphasis added). There was no question in his mind that trials would come. The apostle Peter also told us not to be surprised by our suffering

(1 Peter 4:12-13). Especially in times of great distress, we can come to the point where we simply don't know what to do. This then moves us to the other side of the balance, which is our never-ending need to trust God.

*Sovereignty Over All*

In his helpful book *Trusting God,* Jerry Bridges says there are three things we must believe if we are to trust God in adversity: God is completely sovereign, infinite in wisdom, and perfect in love.[5] In our last chapter we touched on the topic of God's sovereignty in connection to hope, and we will now see its vital importance in relation to trusting Him. Having the confidence as believers that a loving Father is in control of everything makes all the difference in the world. As Maurice Roberts states in *The Thought of God,* "To be told that 'all things work together for good' (Romans 8:28) to us is to have more than a cordial. It is to have the elixir of life."[6] In our modern-day vernacular, the sovereignty of God is the dealbreaker; it is the gamechanger. As we have seen, when we embrace the certainty that all things are being used for our good and His glory, we realize that even the most difficult of situations are still under His complete control. And the assurance of this is what gives us the ongoing strength to strive.

Ponder these encouraging thoughts regarding God's sovereignty and His loving oversight of the smallest details of our lives:

There is nothing—no circumstance, no trouble, no testing—that can ever touch me until first of all it has gone past God and past Christ, right through to me. If it has come that far, it has come with a great purpose, which I may not understand at the moment. But as I refuse to become panicky, as I lift up my eyes to Him and accept it as coming from the throne of God for some great purpose of blessing to my own heart, no sorrow will ever disturb me, no trial will ever disarm me, no circumstance will cause me to fret...[7]

The sovereignty of God is the one impregnable rock to which the suffering human heart must cling. The circumstances surrounding our lives are no accident; they may be the work of evil, but that evil is held firmly within the mighty hand of our sovereign God...All evil is subject to Him, and evil cannot touch His children unless He permits it.[8]

Whatever our particular circumstances may be, Christ assures us that our times are in His hand (Psalm 31:15). We only have to live one day at a time (Matthew 6:34) and He will never give us more than we can bear (1 Corinthians 10:13). We may not be able to make sense of His plan, but that is simply a reminder that we have not yet reached the end of the story.

### The Three Questions

Many years ago my husband and I had a discussion about God's sovereignty that resulted in what we subsequently labeled "the three questions." We have found these questions to be immensely helpful when confronted with challenging situations in our own lives. The first question is this: "Could God have stopped it?" The "it" could refer to a person, an event, or a set of circumstances; it is whatever is causing you frustration, disappointment, pain, or sorrow. And this first question always has the same answer: a resounding yes! God is the sovereign Ruler of the universe. He can do anything He desires (Job 42:2; Psalm 103:19; 115:3). The second question to ask ourselves is: "*Did* He stop it?" This question is a sobering one because, if you are in a trial, the answer is obviously no. God did not stop or change the situation even though He could have. The third question is the most important: "Why not?" Perhaps a better way to state this final question could be, "What is God doing?" Or, "What is He teaching me?"

If you want to learn to trust God more, you *must* come to terms with the profound implications of these three questions. The undeniable truth is that God could have easily prevented or put an end to whatever adversity you might be experiencing—but He sovereignly chose not to. Because we have the promise from Scripture that His way is perfect (Psalm 18:30), we can only conclude that His best and highest purpose is somehow being accomplished *through* this trial instead of the removal of it. Believing this will revolutionize your perspective, not only on how you see your suffering, but how you perceive every aspect of your journey through this life. The overwhelming reality of God's sovereignty becomes the grid through which you view every single circumstance. Even when we are confident that the Lord is in control, unfortunately there are sometimes no easy answers to life's challenges. Yet the most difficult trials are much easier to endure when we acknowledge they are being used in God's economy for good; in fact, embracing the sovereignty of God is sometimes the *only* thing that makes extreme suffering bearable.

One of the chief blessings of resting in God's providence is that it takes away the second-guessing of our choices; it removes the "what-ifs" of our lives that can hold us captive in paralyzing regret of our past decisions. And this regret can keep us from fulfilling our responsibility to strive. As my oldest daughter once gently reminded me, "There are no what ifs; there is only what *is*." And what *is* testifies to His perfect decretive will for us at this moment. Never forget: God could have stopped it. He has the power to do anything. He could have changed our thinking, our perspectives, or the choices that we made. But He *didn't*. And although we may not understand what He's doing, our part is to simply trust that whatever He has chosen is the absolute best for us. And out of that trust, we take necessary steps of action.

### Wisdom Beyond Our Comprehension

As previously mentioned, Bridges explains in his book that another key to trusting God is believing that He is infinite in His wisdom. How can we even begin to comprehend the wisdom of our omniscient, almighty God? As Romans 11:33 exclaims, "Oh, the depth of the riches and wisdom and knowledge of God! How unsearchable are his judgments and how inscrutable his ways!" Psalm 147:5 tells us that "his understanding is beyond measure." The book of Proverbs also marvels at the vast wisdom of the Lord (2:6; 3:19; 8:22-30).

How is it then that we find ourselves so easily question-ing what He has allowed in our lives? Do we truly think we are wiser than He is? As we saw in our last chapter, God's thoughts and ways are immeasurably higher than ours (Isaiah 55:8-9) so it should not be a surprise if they are often perplexing to us. One aspect that may disturb us, and yet is quite clear from Scripture, is that the Lord, in His great wisdom, often uses suffering to accomplish His divine purposes (Psalm 119:67, 71).

Why is this so necessary? Ideally, as believers, we should see steady spiritual growth as the resident Holy Spirit leads us into a deeper knowledge of God and His Word; yet sadly, because of the principle of indwelling sin (Romans 7:23), we are constantly tempted to operate independently of our Lord and pridefully go our own way. It is a hard thing to admit but at times, we *need* adver-sity in our lives. As the old hymn says, we are "prone to wander...prone to leave the God I love."[9] We do love our Savior, yet we are so easily distracted by the attractions of this deceptive world. As explained in chapter 7, when tri-als come our way, they demand our attention and humble us and call us back into repentant, obedient submission to His Word. Suffering is an extremely effective tool in the hands of a wise and loving Father. Real, lasting changes are often hammered out in the midst of great difficulty, and these are the lessons that are never forgotten. Yet there is no doubt that this is the more painful path. How much better it is if we allow ourselves to be constantly broken by God's Word so that it is not necessary for Him to bring hard circumstances into our lives to break us.

The author of Hebrews adds this reassuring perspective: sometimes our difficult circumstances are simply evidence of our Heavenly Father's merciful discipline. As Hebrews 12:6 puts it, "For the Lord disciplines the one he loves." God's ultimate goal in His discipline is our holiness and "the peaceful fruit of righteousness to those who have been trained by it" (Hebrews 12:10-11). The psalmist also affirms that the Lord afflicts us in faithfulness (Psalm 119:75). As Bridges says, "God knows exactly what He intends we become and He knows exactly what circumstances, both good and bad, are necessary to produce that result in our lives."[10] Our Father will do whatever it takes to conform us to the image of His Son (Romans 8:29) because there is no greater good than that. The Lord does not always give us what we *want;* He gives us what we *need.* And no one knows what we need better than the One who created us.

Joni Eareckson Tada encourages us with these insights on God's incredible wisdom and extraordinary providence in our lives:

I tell you, if we could only watch the way God works behind-the-scenes we would have a greatly expanded view of the miraculous. The superbly conceived, delicately balanced, invisible workings of our great God—this is the real drama. Meanwhile he just wants us to trust him…our inability to comprehend something doesn't make it untrue or any less miraculous.[11]

If you are currently struggling to trust the Lord in a particular situation, if you are fighting to believe that He's actually doing the wisest thing in your life, then allow me to remind you of a fellow struggler we find in Scripture. His name was Job, and most would agree that our experiences of suffering pale in comparison to his. He lost his wealth, his livelihood, his children, his health. All that remained to him was a wife who advised him to curse God and die (Job 2:9). In his anguish and despair, we find him demanding answers from the Lord in Job 31: "Oh, that I had one to hear me!...Let the Almighty answer me!" (31: 35) He wanted to know *why* God had allowed these trials in his life. Sound familiar?

The Lord was incredibly patient with Job but finally we hear Him speak these words in Job 38: "Who is this that darkens counsel by words without knowledge? Dress for action like a man; I will question you, and you make it known to me" (38:2-3). In effect, God said "Job, it's my turn now. Let Me ask *you* some questions." God then proceeded to level Job in the next several chapters with a divine inquisition that was totally unanswerable. In Job 38:4-35, we are allowed to eavesdrop on some of the staggering questions that the Lord asked him. Where was Job when God laid the foundation of the earth? Where was he when the Lord filled the mighty oceans and told the waves where they must stop on the beach? Was it Job who commanded the sun to rise every morning? Had he walked in the depths of the sea or seen the gates of death? Did he know where the light and the darkness made their home? Was it Job who had placed the constellations in the night sky? Did the snow and the hail and the rain all answer to him? Did the lightning report to Job to ask where it should strike? The interrogation continued until Job was thoroughly humbled and repentant (Job. 40:3-5; 42:1-3). The overwhelming conclusion of this exchange was that the Lord controlled all these things and Job controlled *none* of them! The Lord never did answer Job's questions; He simply showed him His wisdom and power and His sovereignty over the totality of creation. Job saw his God as he had never seen Him before and that was enough (Job 42:5-6).

We too must humbly learn the same lesson that Job did. Our amazing God oversees *the entire universe*, and He is more than wise enough to oversee our individual lives! He is infinite; we are finite. He is God; we are not. In the end, we don't need to know *why*; we simply need to know God. Jerry Bridges gives us these astute observations on the wisdom of God:

> We are almost insatiable in our quest for the 'why' of the adversity that has come upon us. But this is a futile as well as an untrusting task. God's ways, being the ways of infinite wisdom, simply cannot be comprehended by our finite minds.[12]

We must learn to trust God's character more than our capacity to discern His ways. God does not answer all our questions because we are simply unable to fathom many of His answers.

### The Blessings of Suffering

While we therefore may not always understand why, what we *can* understand from Scripture is that a multitude of benefits result from our suffering. Through our painful afflictions, God is teaching us priceless lessons about the mystery of suffering and its sanctifying role in our lives (Psalm 66:10; 119:67,71; Ecclesiastes 7:3-4; Romans 5:3-4; James 1:2-4; 1 Peter 5:10). He is strengthening our faith (Job 23:10; 1 Peter 1:6-7). Not only is He drawing us into a deeper knowledge of who *He* is, as He did with Job and Paul (Job 42:5, Philippians 3:10), He is also teaching us who *we* are (Deuteronomy 8:2). He is ushering us into a more profound dependence on Him (Psalm 73:25-26,28; 2 Corinthians 12:7-10). He is using our own heartaches to engender in us empathy and compassion for the heartaches of others (2 Corinthians 1:4-5). These blessings are invaluable. Elisabeth Elliot, in sharing about adversity in her life, offers this testimony:

> And I learned in that experience who God is…in a way that I could never have known otherwise. And so I can say to you that suffering is an irreplaceable medium through which I learned an indispensable truth.[13]

### Amazing, Boundless Love

In *Trusting God*, Bridges' final prerequisite to trusting God is believing that He is perfect in love. We acknowledge that God is completely sovereign. We bow to His infinite wisdom. But if we are to trust Him, it is also crucial that we grasp just how deeply He loves us. We are told in Scripture that the Lord loves us with an everlasting love (Jeremiah 31:3) and it will never be removed from us (Isaiah 54:10). He loved His people so much that while we were yet sinners, He sent His only Son Jesus to die for us and save us from our sin (Romans 5:8; John 3:16; 15:13). Because of His great love, He has made us alive together with Christ and seated us with Him in heavenly places so that He can show us His love forever (Ephesians 2:4-7). His love grants us eternal comfort and good hope through grace (2 Thessalonians 2:16) and nothing will ever separate us from His love (Romans 8:35-39).

When we are in the midst of a painful experience of suffering, it is easy to lose sight of this amazing love that our Lord has for us. This is why it is so essential that we ground our minds in Scripture. We rehearse what is *true* and cling to it with everything we have. Shaking off our doubts, we remember what He has done (Psalm 77:11-15; 103:2-6). We talk to ourselves and remind ourselves where our hope is found (Psalm 42:5,11). We do not look to our temporal circumstances for proof of God's love; this is a broken world that is full of sorrow and heartache and death because of the effects of sin. If we want to be reassured of God's love, we must look to our precious Lord Jesus and His sacrificial death for us on the cross. This is a picture of supreme love that will never dim. The fact is, when a believer is wrestling with anger toward God because of their circumstances, the root problem is that they are struggling to believe that their Father loves them. When we truly perceive the depth of His love for us, this will enable us to trust Him wholeheartedly, even in the most difficult of situations.

Anna L. Waring, a Welsh hymn-writer in the 1800's, had a deep sense of God's love and knew the profound difference it made in her trials:

In heav'nly love abiding, no change my heart shall fear;
And safe is such confiding for nothing changes here.
The storm may roar without me, my heart may low be laid,
But God is round about me, and can I be dismayed?[14]

## THE TRUSTING LIFE

*Study, Study, Study*

What then should be seen in our lives as we seek to trust Him more? First of all, a commitment to study. As discussed in our last chapter, we *must* spend time in the Word of God (Joshua 1:8; Psalm 119:15; 2 Timothy 2:15). We continually store up truth in our hearts so it is waiting there when the difficulties come. A Bible teacher once told me that Bibles that are falling apart usually belong to people who are *not*! We must be people of the Word. This is how we assimilate theology and other key doctrines. But most of all, this is how we come to personally know and trust God. Proverbs 22:17-19 gives insight into a fundamental goal of studying Scripture and the wisdom of God, "...that your trust may be in the Lord..." We want to grow in our knowledge of God's Word because this enables us to know the God of the Word in a deeper, more intimate way. And the more we come to know Him, the more we will trust Him.

We should also read good books: books that aid us in our study of Scripture, books that address substantial issues in Christianity, and also books that focus on the attributes of God. Written material that helps us comprehend more about God's perfections is critical since it will help us develop a high view of Him, which in turn will lead to more trust and more worship. Holding a high view of God is important because our problems are relative.

People who struggle with fear often have a low view of God and their problems seem overwhelming in comparison. But when we have a high view of God, He takes away our fear and our problems become smaller (Deuteronomy 31:8; Psalm 27:1; Isaiah 41:10,13; 2 Timothy 1:7).

We must also listen to the Word taught and preached faithfully by pastors and elders. The more we can fill our minds with biblical truth, the more equipped we are to deal with the challenges of this world. Being a committed member of a local church body, therefore, is imperative if we are going to place ourselves under the regular ministry of the scriptures. Whatever church you may attend, make certain that the teaching of the Word is central, not peripheral.

*Pray Without Ceasing*

As we endeavor to trust God, something else that should be very evident in our lives is faithful, fervent prayer. It is a natural response that the more helpless we feel, the more we will entreat our Heavenly Father in prayer. When the unbelieving world experiences trials and tribulations, they run any number of places to try to find relief from their suffering. But we are God's children, and when we are in distress, we run to *Him* (Psalm 46:1-2; 71:1-3; 121:1-3).

Although Scripture regularly commands us to pray, many believers would sadly confess that prayer is the weakest link in their spiritual chain. Yet, as we saw in chapter 7, it is an indispensable element of our Christian walk (Colossians 4:2; 1 Thessalonians 5:17). J. C. Ryle cautions us to "watch our habits of prayer with a holy watchfulness. Here is the pulse of our Christianity. Here is the true test of our state before God."[15] Alistair Begg comments on our desperate need to seek God's face in prayer:

> My prayers—whether I pray, how much I pray, about what I pray—reveal my priorities...If Paul, "an apostle of Christ Jesus by the will of God" (Ephesians 1:1), knew that he needed to "bow my knees before the Father" (3:4), what of us? If Jesus Christ, the greatest teacher in the world, followed up his instruction by prayer, what of us? If Jesus Christ, who was set on a mission that changed not just world history but all of eternity, took time to pray, what of us? If Jesus Christ, the Son of God, knew that he needed to pray, what of us?[16]

What is prayer? The Westminster Shorter Catechism defines it as "an offering up of our desires unto God, for things agreeable to His will, in the name of Christ, with confession of our sins and thankful acknowledgement of His mercies."[17] Maurice Roberts gives this wonderfully simple explanation: "Prayer is the natural response of a converted heart to an inner desire for communion with God."[18] Joel Beeke and Joel Najapfour convey some of John Calvin's timeless thoughts on the priority of prayer:

> In prayer we both communicate and commune with our Father in heaven...Like Christ in Gethsemane, we cast our desires, sighs, anxieties, fears, hopes, and joys into the lap of God...We are permitted to pour into God's bosom the difficulties which torment us, in order that He may loosen the

knots which we cannot untie…Prayer is the most important part of the Christian life; it is the life-blood of every true believer.[19]

John Calvin wrote these words in the 1500s, yet today we still cry out to God about our deep heartaches and "the knots which we cannot untie." So prayer should be a priority in our lives as we trust the Lord. In Psalm 62, we find the exhortation to trust God inseparably linked to pouring our hearts out before Him: "Trust in him at all times, O people; pour out your heart before him; God is a refuge for us" (62:8).

One of the privileges we have as believers is being able to carry our burdens to the Lord and roll them onto Him (Psalm 55:22); we pray for help to live holy, obedient lives (Psalm 66:18; James 5:16); we confidently take our petitions to the Father in prayer and supplication with thanksgiving (Philippians 4:6-7; Hebrews 4:16); and then we wait patiently. We know He is sovereign, yet we still bring Him our requests because, as D.A. Carson reminds us, "the Bible simultaneously pictures God as utterly sovereign and also as a prayer-hearing, prayer-answering God."[20] We pray for God's will and glory, we pray for others, and we pray for ourselves. And even when we don't receive an immediate answer or the answer we want, we trust that He is at work. We ultimately find our comfort in *who He is*. He hears us, He is good, and He will always do what is right. Prayer keeps us from losing heart (Luke 18:1).

For those of you who are parents, I beseech you to pray faithfully for your children. Intercede for them before the throne of God! There is nothing more powerful that you can do than pray for your children as they grow to adulthood.

And even after they are adults, continue to uplift them in prayer. Pray for their spiritual state. Pray they will love God and His Word. Pray for their character. I encourage every parent to keep a prayer journal and create an individual section for each child. As you pray over the course of many years, jot down short records of what you are praying. And someday, when your children leave home, present them with their prayer pages. You have essentially written a diary of their entire lives as seen through the eyes of a praying mother or father. We may fail in many ways as parents, but the Lord will honor your prayers for your children.

A wonderful old hymn, *Come, My Soul, With Every Care*, reminds us of the great King who holds court with us each time we pray and explains why we can approach Him with "large petitions":

> You are coming to a King
> Large petitions with you bring
> For His grace and pow'r are such
> None can ever ask too much[21]

John Bunyan once said, "You can do more than pray, after you have prayed, but you cannot do more than pray, until you have prayed."[22] We are given this encouragement from S. D. Gordon: "The greatest thing anyone can do for God and for man is to pray. It is not the only thing. But it is the chief thing."[23] We would do well to heed their wise words.

### *It's Your Choice*

In addition to studying and praying, another vital ingredient is *choosing* to trust Him. Trusting God is not a matter of my feelings but of my *will*. The Holy Spirit that lives in me can enable me to make right choices, and thus I can decide to trust the Lord even when I don't *feel* like it. In every trial, the ultimate question is always whether we will choose to trust Him. We either will or we won't. In 1 Peter, we are exhorted with these words to make that right choice: "Therefore let those who suffer according to God's will *entrust their souls* to a faithful Creator" (4:19, emphasis added).

Throughout Scripture, we are introduced to many individuals who chose to trust when enduring affliction. One Old Testament example is found in the book of Habakkuk. God had revealed to the prophet that Israel would soon be judged severely by a wicked enemy nation. Habakkuk's complete way of life was about to be destroyed and ripped from him. Yet we hear his hopeful words in Habakkuk 3:17-18, and we see the choice he made to trust God despite his circumstances:

Though the fig tree should not blossom, nor fruit be on the vines...[though] the flock be cut off from the fold and there be no herd in the stalls, yet I will rejoice in the LORD; I will take joy in the God of my salvation.

In 1 Peter, we are shown another portrait of someone who made the choice to trust in the midst of great suffering—and this is the supreme example of our precious Lord Jesus. He has given us His pattern to follow:

For to this you have been called, because Christ also suffered for you, leaving you an example, so that you might follow in his steps. He committed no sin, neither was deceit found in his mouth. When he was reviled, he did not revile in return; when he suffered, he did not threaten, but continued entrusting himself to him who judges justly. (2:21-23)

## *The Surrender That Frees Us*

As we conclude, we must realize that a crucial component of trusting God is total surrender to His will. And there are very few things we will ever do that are more difficult. Even when we love Christ and belong to Him, our flesh periodically pushes us to fight for control of the wheel so we can try to steer our own course. Oswald Chambers provides us with this valuable insight:

Surrender is not the surrender of the external life but of the will; when that is done, all is done. There are very few crises in life; the great crisis is the surrender of the will.[24]

Trusting God means learning to offer up *everything* to Him—all that we are and all that we have, and especially the things that are the most precious to us. For those of us who are parents, probably one of our most difficult challenges is our children. We are accustomed to protecting them and it is hard to completely entrust them to the Lord when we have no idea what that might entail. A.W. Tozer speaks to this struggle:

We are often hindered from giving our treasures to the Lord out of fear for their safety; this is especially true when those treasures are loved relatives and friends. But we need have no such fears...Everything is safe which we commit to Him, and nothing is really safe which is not so committed.[25]

There is an amazing sense of relief that comes when we place the people we cherish in the safekeeping of God. We should never deceive ourselves into thinking they are ultimately our responsibility; they are His, and always have been. Especially with our children, we must strive to be the very best parents we can possibly be; we must give it all that we have. But we can never forget they don't really belong to us. They ultimately belong to Him and we are only their stewards for a short time. We find our rest, though, in the assurance that their times are also "in His hand" (Psalm 31:15) and so in the end—we trust.

We *must* give everything to God. There really is no other choice if we want to know peace. In John 6, many of Jesus' followers had left Him and He asked his disciples if they would also go away. Peter's poignant words in verse 68 pierce deep in our hearts, "Lord, to whom shall we go?" Here is the profound truth: there is no one else to go to *but* Him (Isaiah 45:5-6; Acts 4:12; 1 Corinthians 8:6).

I have always loved the old Irish hymn "Be Thou My Vision." In the last verse, we find these words: "Heart of my own heart, *whatever befall*" (emphasis added). Here we see a picture of total surrender. Whatever comes, whatever our lot, it matters not—we will still trust Him. Spurgeon affirms this when he encourages us to cultivate "unstaggering trustfulness in our God, the confidence which we have in Him that He will neither do us ill Himself, nor suffer anyone else to harm us…If the very worst should happen, our God is still the greatest and best. The Lord liveth, and what can his children fear?"[26]

Our God *can* be trusted. He draws us out of many waters (Psalm 18:16); He lifts us up out of the pit and sets our feet upon a rock (Psalm 40:1-3); He rescues us from the depths when we call to Him (Psalm 130:1-2). In Psalm 107, we find the story of a great storm at sea and the mighty Deliverer who hears the desperate cry of the sailors and rescues them. Martyn Lloyd-Jones reflects on this psalm and on the Savior we can put our confidence in:

> [W]hen in the midst of life you feel you are about to sink, but then you meet Christ, you feel at once that here is somebody who knows, here is somebody who understands. Here is someone who has faced the storm at its most desperate, with all the billows of hell howling at Him; but He went through them all and came to the haven successfully. He has stepped on board. He is in control. He understands. He knows what He's doing.[27]

## THE RESULTS OF TRUST

When we do make the right choice, what are the results of our trust? First and foremost, it honors and glorifies God (Psalm 40:3; 1 Corinthians 10:31). We are telling the world that He *can* be trusted. Ian Hamilton instructs us here:

Those believers whose faith most glorifies God are...those who humbly trust God when all around their soul is giving way. God's ways are not our ways. He is God. His purposes towards his people are the product of his perfect wisdom, gracious sovereignty and electing love...The quiet dignity of a bruised reed, humbled under God's almighty hand, is a beautiful sight to behold. It is a testimony to the grace and love of an unseen God. It tells the people of God that God can be trusted, even when all earthly hopes are dashed.[28]

When we choose to trust, not only does it glorify God, it also brings joy and peace to our lives (Psalm 33:21; Jeremiah 17:7). We will know a joy that is far too deep to be disturbed:

Christian joy is the emotion springing from the deep-down confidence of the Christian that God is in complete and perfect control of everything, and will bring from it our good in time, and our glory in eternity...Christian joy is not an emotion on top of an emotion. It is not a feeling on top of a feeling. It is a feeling on top of a fact. It is an emotional response to what I know to be true about my God.[29]

We will also know peace. Isaiah 26:3 promises, "You keep him in perfect peace whose mind is stayed on you, because he trusts in you." What does peace look like? Psalm 131:2 gives us a picture: "But I have calmed and quieted my soul, like a weaned child with its mother; like a weaned child is my soul within me." This psalm came to mind recently as I held my young grandson and read some of his favorite books to him. As he sat in my lap, quiet and content, I was reminded of how the Lord longs for us to rest in His arms in just that way and trust Him. When His will becomes *our* will, peace is the result. Ponder this wise counsel to "lie quiet" under His hand:

> Neither go back in fear and misgiving to the past, nor in anxiety and forecasting to the future, but lie quiet under His hand, having no will but His.[30]

## THE FREEDOM TO TRY

Returning to our balance, we must understand that God grants us the freedom to strive to fulfill our responsibilities. In any situation we face, some level of action on our part is required. We must make choices to gather information, attack problems, find solutions, resolve difficulties, and so on. But what if we don't make the perfect choices in our striving? What if we fail? It is the comfort we derive from trusting the Lord that frees us from these fears, for we know that He overturns our mistakes, and even our sin, to still accomplish His will. So we keep trusting, and we keep striving, all at the same time.

## IT'S ALL UP TO ME

Let us turn our attention now to the two sides of this balance and see what dangers lurk in the extremes. If we tend to be like Martha and spend most of our life striving and staying busy, what are the symptoms that might surface? Probably the chief concern is the reliance on self that can develop over time. In practical matters, we can become so accustomed to taking things into our own hands that we mistakenly begin to believe that we really *are* in control. We can develop a habit of depending solely on ourselves instead of humbly asking direction from the Lord in our endeavors. This mindset can also push us toward becoming more controlling of situations and other people as we attempt to eliminate the variables that would prevent us from reaching the goals we are so determined to achieve. In the spiritual realm, we can fall into the "works-righteousness" trap of thinking we have to earn points with God and somehow impress Him with our performance. Like Martha, we can get so distracted by our service that we virtually forget our communion with our Lord. Anxiety and fear are the logical side effects of this pressure of feeling like it's all up to us. As we rely on our own strength and desperately try to keep all the plates spinning, we can find it harder and harder to humbly submit to the Lord's providence in our lives.

## IT'S ALL UP TO HIM

On the other side of the balance, can we trust Him too much? No, not literally. But there is still a danger to avoid. We must not allow our dependence on God to result in laziness toward spiritual things and the commands of Scripture that call us to action. When we don't want to do the preparation necessary to mature as a Christian but simply want God to sprinkle some sort of magic dust on us to instantly make us spiritually mature, we are out of balance. As we have seen, there are key spiritual disciplines such as Bible study and prayer that we need to actively pursue in our lives rather than being passive. As we study Scripture, we must obey the commands and exhortations we find there. Our responsibilities to our families, churches, and communities are clearly outlined in the Word, and we need to actively minister to those around us. When we put no effort whatsoever into these things and yet expect the Lord to constantly "bail us out" when we are in difficult situations, this is nothing less than presumption on Him. Our God is exceedingly gracious and kind to His undeserving creatures, yet the bottom line is that He does not owe us anything. We must therefore be careful to never presume on His goodness.

We have previously addressed the danger of mysticism, and once again this is a temptation for the person who doesn't want to put in the time and effort required to grow spiritually or to address life's concerns. Mysticism is characterized by living the Christian life subjectively rather than objectively; it is expressed in basing our decisions primarily on feelings and personal experience rather than the truth of God's Word. It's much easier to say, "I *feel* like I should do this," rather than engage in the hard work of actually determining what God *said* I should do. Maturity (spiritual or otherwise) is a process that takes time. If we are genuinely regenerate, the indwelling Holy Spirit is our teacher, and we must be diligent students. It requires disciplined mental effort as we think, evaluate, meditate, pray, and dialogue on any number of issues. The "let go and let God" mentality offers a superficial approach to life and basically eliminates the legitimate striving that is an essential element of our journey. There are no quick fixes in the believer's life. After salvation, a certain amount of reasonable and consistent effort is undeniably required as we seek to live wise and holy lives for God's glory. We must not shirk our responsibility to face challenges head on and determine the wisest course of action. And as we fulfill that responsibility, we continue to trust God every step of the way.

## THE EXTREMES

When we lose our balance, then, in this area of striving and trusting, what does it look like? If you are overly focused on *striving*, these symptoms may manifest themselves in your life:

- Self-confidence/self-sufficiency
- "Works–righteousness"
- Anxiety/fear

If you are too extreme in your emphasis on *trusting*, here are the possible dangers:

- Laziness/passivity/presumption on God
- Mysticism
- "Let go and let God" mentality

In summary, we work, and God works. We do everything we know to do, all the while trusting Him for the results. Just as I put my complete trust in my earthly father so many years ago, even more so I must trust my Heavenly Father. He is the Divine Pilot. I am safe with Him.

# *For Personal Reflection and Application*

## CHAPTER 8—STRIVING AND TRUSTING

1. In the area of our sanctification, God has ordained that His children have a role to play. In Proverbs 2:1-7 and 3:5-8, what are we told to do? What does God promise to do in these verses? How does Philippians 2:12-13 help you stay balanced in the pursuit of spiritual growth?

2. In 1 Corinthians 3:6-7, what was Paul's perspective toward his ministry? What dangers can result if we do not maintain an attitude of humble dependence on God as we serve others?

3. According to Colossians 1:29, how are believers to accomplish good works? List the good works that we find in the following passages: Colossians 1:10-12; 3:12-17; 1 Thessalonians 5:12-21; and 1 Timothy 6:11-14.

4. God in His wisdom often allows suffering in our lives to bring about great good. What are some of the benefits of our trials? (Deuteronomy 8:2,16; Job 23:10; Romans 5:3; 2 Corinthians 1:4-5; 4:17; Philippians 3:10; James 1:2-4; 1 Peter 1:6-7; 5:10) Which of these have you personally experienced in your own life?

5.  In his book *Trusting God*, Jerry Bridges says that in order to trust God, we must believe He is completely sovereign, infinite in wisdom, and perfect in love. Do you struggle with any of these areas? If so, which ones?

6.  Taking time to study and meditate on God's attributes is immensely helpful in learning to trust Him. What are some of the aspects of God's character that are the most encouraging to you personally? Give some examples of how these attributes have helped you to trust Him in difficult situations.

# ENDNOTES

1   Adams, E. (2018). "Getting on a Plane? Here's How They're Inspected to Keep You Safe." *Popular Science* (May 22). https://www.popsci.com/faa-commercial-airline-plane-inspections/.

2   Johnston, M. (2018). "Airplane Preflight." *CALAERO Blog* (May 24). https://calaero.edu/airplane-preflight-checklist/.

3   Got Questions. "Who were Sanballat, Tobiah, and Geshem?" https://www.gotquestions.org/Sanballat-Tobiah-Geshem.html. Accessed June 21, 2020.

4   Spurgeon, C. (2003). *Morning and Evening* (January 24, evening) (Wheaton, IL: Crossway).

5   Bridges, J. (1988). *Trusting God: Even When Life Hurts* (Colorado Springs, CO: NavPress), 18.

6   Roberts, M. (1995). *The Thought of God* (Carlisle, PA: The Banner of Truth Trust), 6.

7   AZ Quotes. "Alan Redpath Quotes." https://www.azquotes.com/author/24224-Alan_Redpath. Accessed June 26, 2020.

8   Clarkson, M. (1985). *Grace Grows Best in Winter* (Grand Rapids, MI: Wm. B. Eerdmans), 40–41.

9   Robinson, R. (1758). "Come Thou Fount of Every Blessing." Public Domain.

10  Bridges. *Trusting God,* 121.

11 Tada, J. E. (2010). *A Place of Healing* (Colorado Springs, CO: David C. Cook), 60–61.

12 Bridges. *Trusting God,* 125–26.

13 Elliot, E. (2019). *Suffering is Never for Nothing* (Nashville, TN: B&H Publishing Group), 15.

14 The Elisabeth Elliot Newsletter, May/June 1994, elisabethelliot.org/newsletters/may-june-94.pdf.

15 Ryle, J. C. (2020). *Expository Thoughts on the Gospel of Mark: A Commentary* (Abbotsford, WI: Aneko Press), 14.

16 Begg, A. (2019). *Pray Big: Learn to Pray Like an Apostle* (The Good Book Company), 22.

17 Westminster Shorter Catechism Project, Question 98. https://www.shortercatechism.com/resources/wsc/wsc_098.html. Accessed June 29, 2020.

18 Roberts, M. https://mauriceroberts.org/blog/2017/8/28/getting-started-in-prayer

19 Beeke, J., and Najapfour, B. (2011). *Taking Hold of God: Reformed and Puritan Perspectives on Prayer* (Grand Rapids, MI: Reformation Heritage Books), 29.

20 Carson, D. A. (1992). *Spiritual Reformation* (Ada, MI: Baker Academic; Reprint edition), 31.

21 Newton, J. "Come, My Soul, With Every Care."

22 Grace Quotes. "John Bunyan." https://gracequotes.org/author-quote/john-bunyan/. Accessed June 30, 2020.

23 Christian Quotes. "S. D. Gordon." http://christian-quotes.ochristian.com/S.D.-Gordon-Quotes/. Accessed June 29, 2020.

24 Chambers, O. (1935). *My Utmost for His Highest* (September 13) (Toronto, ON: McClelland and Stewart Limited).

25 Tozer, A. W. (1993). *The Pursuit of God* (Camp Hill, PA: Christian Publications, Inc.), 28.

26 Spurgeon, C. (1996). *The Cheque Book of the Bank of Faith* (Geanies House, Fearn, Ross-shire: Great Britain: Christian Focus Publications), 58.

27 Lloyd-Jones, M. (2001). *True Happiness: Psalm 1 and 107* (Wheaton, IL: Crossway), 159.

28 Hamilton, I. (2015). *The Faith-Shaped Life* (Carlisle, PA: The Banner of Truth Trust), 108.

29 MacArthur, J. "Grace to You." https://www.gty.org/resources/pdf/sermons, 52–57. Accessed June 27, 2020.

30 Elliot, E. (1995). *Keep A Quiet Heart* (Ann Arbor, MI: Servant Publications), 147.

*Therefore…let us also lay aside every encumbrance and the sin which so easily entangles us, and let us run with endurance the race that is set before us, fixing our eyes on Jesus, the author and perfecter of faith…*
—Hebrews 12:1-2 (NASB)

# CONCLUSION

We must understand that navigating through this world is much like walking a tightrope. As we traverse this narrow thread we call life, we are acutely aware of the dangers that lay all around us. When we err and go to the extreme in some area of life, the results can be disastrous—mentally, emotionally, physically, and spiritually. The consequences of our own choices can lead us to frustration, despair, and hopelessness. However, there is a foundational secret to every successful tightrope performance: when you're on the wire, you must keep your balance.[1]

If you've ever witnessed a high-wire act, you have noticed the "balancing pole," a long, heavy pole the performers always hold in their hands. The properties of this pole enable the artists to greatly increase their stability on the wire and keep their balance. It helps to keep them centered and steady and protects them against external forces such as a sudden gust of wind. The pole is not an optional piece of equipment but instead is absolutely essential to the performers' success and safety. As Christians, we must realize that amidst the pressures and gusty winds of this earthly life, we too have something that keeps us stable, and that is the holy Word of God! It is God-breathed (2 Timothy 3:16) and therefore without error; it is living and active, piercing to the deepest part of us (Hebrews 4:12) and therefore sufficient; it is eternal and will never pass away (Isaiah 40:8, Mark 13:31) and therefore our timeless authority. The truth and wisdom that we find in the living Word (Christ) and the written Word (Scripture) are what keep us balanced in an unbalanced world. Moreover, as we saw in the Introduction, there has never existed a more perfect picture of balance than our Savior, the Lord Jesus Christ. Jonathan Edwards echoes this thought:

> Truly holy affections in a saint are balanced. This is the dominant trait of their sanctity. The whole image of Christ is impressed upon them...there is in Him every grace; and He is full of grace and truth.[2]

As we journey through life, perhaps the most astounding thing of all is that in spite of our sin, we can actually become more like Jesus Christ! At the moment of regeneration, we are given the wonderful gift of the indwelling Holy Spirit, our ever-present Helper who teaches and convicts us, who comforts and guides us (John 14:26). God tells us that He has started a good work in us that He will complete (Philippians 1:6) and we can be sure He is always at work to conform us to the image of His Son (Romans 8:29). Lastly, we have a precious promise in the book of 2 Corinthians that as we gaze with our spiritual eyes at who Christ is, as we behold the glory of the Lord, the Spirit is actually transforming us into His likeness, little by little.

> And we all, with unveiled face, beholding the glory of the Lord, are being transformed into the same image from one degree of glory to another. (3:18)

As we close, I want to leave you with a fitting postscript about the Wallenda family. Karl, the patriarch, died in a fall in 1978 in Puerto Rico. Karl's great-grandson is a man named Nik Wallenda, who has gained recognition in recent years for crossing high wires over landmarks such as the Grand Canyon, Niagara Falls, downtown Chicago, and Times Square in New York City.

However, who I really want to tell you about is one of Karl's grandsons, a man named Tino Wallenda. Tino and his wife and children have continued the family tradition, performing their amazing act all over the world. In fact, in 1998, they went back to Detroit where, as an eleven-year-old boy, Tino watched his father fall to his death. Tino and his family went back thirty-six years later to the exact same arena and successfully performed the three-level pyramid. As Tino would say later, they wanted to show that "disaster does not have to end in defeat."

Tino boldly professes his faith in Jesus Christ, and many years ago he wrote an article called "He Found Me" in a Christian magazine. This is what he said:

> When I was seven years old, my grandfather, Karl Wallenda, put me on a wire two feet off the ground. He taught me all the elementary skills: how to hold

my body...how to place my feet...how to hold the pole. But the most important thing that my grand–father taught me was that I needed to focus my attention on a point at the other end of the wire. I need a point to concentrate on to keep me balanced.

The ultimate focus of my life is Jesus Christ. The Bible says that we need to focus our eyes on a fixed point. We need to fix our eyes on Jesus, the Author and Perfecter of our faith (Hebrews 12:2).

At one time or another I have taken each of my four children...on my shoulders as I have walked across the wire. In those situations the children really can't do any balancing; I'm the one who has to balance and support them.

People have asked them "Aren't you scared?" "No," they have said. And when they have been asked, "Why aren't you scared?" they have answered "Because that's my daddy." They have confidence in me because I'm their daddy.

And I have confidence in my heavenly Father. I know that He will take me all the way across this Chasm of Life until I meet Him face to face.[3]

My prayer for each one of us is that as we walk across this "Chasm of Life" as Tino calls it, the Lord will keep us balanced through His Holy Word and by the power of His Spirit enable us to live lives that will bring glory to Him.

*…whatever you do, do all to the glory of God.*
—1 Corinthians 10:31

*Now to him who is able to keep you from*
*stumbling…to the only God, our Savior,*
*through Jesus Christ our Lord, be glory,*
*majesty, dominion, and authority,*
*before all time and now and forever. Amen.*
—Jude 24-25

# ENDNOTES

1   Flayhart, B. (2002). "The Church of the Flying Wallendas." Oak Mountain Presbyterian Church (August 18). http://www.ompd.org/2002/081802.htm.

2   Edwards, J. (1984). *Religious Affections* (Portland, OR: Multnomah Press), 157–58.

3   Wallenda, T. (1999). "He Found Me." *Decision Magazine* (April), 6–7. ©Billy Graham Evangelistic Association, used by permission, all rights reserved.

# WHAT DOES IT MEAN TO BE A CHRISTIAN?

Many different opinions exist about the definition of the word "Christian." But since the term originated in the Bible (Acts 11:26)—what does Scripture say?

A Christian is *not* someone who simply gives mental assent to the existence of God or some type of "higher power." Countless people acknowledge God and yet He makes no discernible difference in their decisions or in how they live their lives. Just remember—the Bible tells us that even the demons (who hate God) believe, and they tremble (James 2:19). *Intellectual belief is not salvation.*

A Christian is *not* someone who simply attends church or tries to do good deeds and live a moral life. All these things may be done for a variety of reasons and be completely independent of a genuine relationship with God. The Bible clearly explains our self-righteous deeds can never secure our salvation (Isaiah 64:6; Titus 3:4-7). *Moral or practical goodness is not salvation.*

According to the Bible, a Christian is one who:

- Acknowledges that he/she is a sinner before a holy, righteous God and that eternal salvation cannot be obtained by any merit or good works on the part of the sinner, but only by God's grace (Ephesians 2:8-9)

- Believes the facts of the gospel: that Jesus Christ is God, and that He came to earth, took on human nature, lived a perfect life, died on the cross to pay the price for sin, and was bodily resurrected on the third day

- Comes in humble repentance and faith, trusting only in Jesus Christ's perfect life, and in His death on the cross to atone for their sin—and nothing else (Acts 4:12; Galatians 2:16)

- After salvation, manifests the fruit of being a new creation in Christ (2 Corinthians 5:17-18): a transformed mind that results in new desires and motivations, submission to Christ as Lord, love for God and His Word, delight in the things of God, and the worship of God rather than self

If you wish to know more about what it means to be a Christian, please see these excellent resources:

Fabarez, Mike (2014). *Exploring the Gospel: Being Sure You're Right with God* (Laguna Hills,CA: Focal Point Ministries)

Gilbert, Greg (2010). *What is the Gospel?* (Wheaton, IL: Crossway)

Blanchard, John (2014). *Ultimate Questions* (Carlisle, PA: Evangelical Press)

*Counsel with Confidence* by Joel James

*Expository Listening* by Ken Ramey

*Glorifying God* by Patti Hummel

*Uneclipsing the Son* by Rick Holland

*The Faith-Shaped Life* by Ian Hamilton

*Free to Be Holy* by Jerry Wragg and Paul Shirley

*Precious Truths in Practice* by Martha Peace

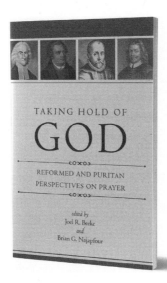

*Taking Hold of God* by Joel Beeke

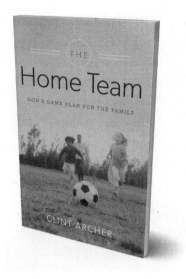

*The Home Team* by Clint Archer

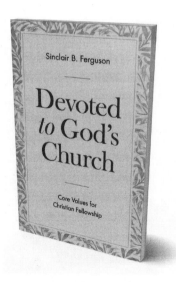

*Devoted to God's Church* by Sinclair Ferguson

*A Lifetime of Wisdom* by Joni Eareckson Tada

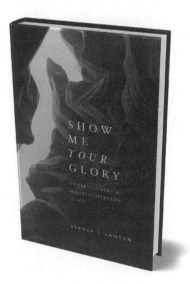

*Show Me Your Glory* by Steve Lawson

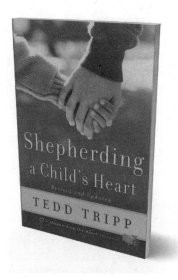

*Shepherding a Child's Heart* by Tedd Tripp